This trademark is owned by the Smithsonian Institution
and is registered in the U.S. Patent and Trademark Office.

SMITHSONIAN INSTITUTION

Established in 1846, the Smithsonian Institution—the world's largest
museum and research complex—includes 19 museums and
galleries and the National Zoological Park. The total number of
artifacts, works of art, and specimens in the Smithsonian's collection
is estimated at 137 million, the bulk of which is contained in
the National Museum of Natural History, which holds more than
126 million specimens and objects. The Smithsonian is a renowned
research center, dedicated to public education, national service,
and scholarship in the arts, sciences, and history.

DK · SMITHSONIAN

THE ELEMENTS BOOK

A VISUAL ENCYCLOPEDIA OF THE PERIODIC TABLE

WRITTEN BY **TOM JACKSON**
CONSULTANT **JACK CHALLONER**

DK Penguin
Random
House

DK India

Senior Editor Bharti Bedi
Project Art Editor Amit Verma
Editorial team Neha Ruth Samuel,
Charvi Arora, Deeksha Saikia
Art Editors Mansi Agrawal, Amisha Gupta, Ravi Indiver
Assistant Art Editors Neetika Malik Jhingan, Nidhi Rastogi
Jacket Designer Suhita Dharamjit
Jackets Editorial Coordinator Priyanka Sharma
Senior DTP Designer Harish Aggarwal
DTP Designers Sachin Gupta, Syed Md Farhan,
Nityanand Kumar, Mohammad Rizwan
Picture Researcher Nishwan Rasool
Managing Jackets Editors Saloni Singh, Sreshtha Bhattacharya
Picture Research Manager Taiyaba Khatoon
Pre-production Manager Balwant Singh
Production Manager Pankaj Sharma
Managing Editor Kingshuk Ghoshal
Managing Art Editor Govind Mittal

DK UK

Project Editor Ashwin Khurana
Senior Art Editor Smiljka Surla
US Senior Editor Margaret Parrish
US Editor Jill Hamilton
Jacket Editor Claire Gell
Senior Jacket Designer Mark Cavanagh
Jacket Design Development Manager Sophia MTT
Managing Editor Lisa Gillespie
Managing Art Editor Owen Peyton Jones
Producers, Pre-production Dragana Puvacic, Catherine Williams
Producer Anna Vallarino
Publisher Andrew Macintyre
Art Director Karen Self
Associate Publishing Director Liz Wheeler
Design Director Phil Ormerod
Publishing Director Jonathan Metcalf

Photographer Ruth Jenkinson
Photography Assistant Julie Stewart

Element samples prepared and supplied by RGB Research Ltd
www.periodictable.co.uk

First American Edition, 2017
Published in the United States by DK Publishing
1450 Broadway, Suite 801, New York, NY 10018

Copyright © 2017 Dorling Kindersley Limited
DK, a Division of Penguin Random House LLC
21 22 13 12
044–289022–Apr/2017

A catalog record for this book is available
from the Library of Congress.
ISBN: 978-1-4654-5660-1

DK books are available at special discounts when purchased in
bulk for sales promotions, premiums, fund-raising, or educational use.
For details, contact: DK Publishing Special Markets,
1450 Broadway, Suite 801, New York, NY 10018
SpecialSales@dk.com

Printed and bound in China

All images © Dorling Kindersley Limited
For further information see: www.dkimages.com

For the curious
www.dk.com

MIX
Paper from
responsible sources
FSC™ C018179

This book was made with Forest Stewardship
Council ™ certified paper — one small step
in DK's commitment to a sustainable future.
For more information go to
www.dk.com/our-green-pledge

CONTENTS

Chunk of yttrium

Chunk of silver

Zirconium crystal bar

Foreword

Everything in nature, from the mountains and oceans to the air we breathe and food we eat are made up of simple substances called elements. You may have already heard of several of them, including gold, iron, oxygen, and helium, but these are just four out of a total of 118. Many have unique—and sometimes surprising—chemical and physical properties. Gallium, for example, is a solid but melts in your hand. A compound of sulfur gives off a unpleasant smell of rotten eggs. Fluorine is a gas that can burn a hole straight through concrete!

The elements are rarely found in their pure form. Mostly, they are combined with each other to make compounds, which make up substances around us. For example, hydrogen and oxygen make water, sodium and chlorine form salt, and carbon is found in millions of compounds, many of which—including proteins and sugars—make our bodies work.

To find out more about the elements, we need to take a good look at the periodic table. This is used by scientists around the world to list and detail the elements. It shows the key information

Nickel balls

Cube of melting gallium

Iodine in a glass sphere

Barium crystals

Chunk of gray selenium

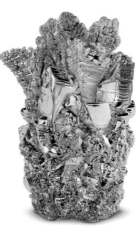

Magnesium crystals

Osmium pellet

for each element, grouping them into similar types. With this information, we can use the elements to make many things we need: a fluorine compound in toothpastes toughens our teeth and silicon crystals engineered into microchips operate our gadgets and phones.

Every element has its own story of where it comes from, what it can do, and how we use it. Let's begin a tour of every element one by one. It's going to be a fascinating journey.

Tom Jackson

	Throughout this book you will find boxes with the following symbols. This is what each of them means.
	This shows the structure of an atom of an element, with the nucleus (made of protons and neutrons) at the center and electrons surrounding it in their shells.
⊖	Electron
⊕	Proton
◯	Neutron
State	The state of the element at a temperature of 68°F (20°C). It can be a solid, liquid, or gas.
Discovery	This details the year in which the element was discovered.

Chunk of uranium

Gold crystals

Thulium crystals

Calcium crystals

Elemental building blocks

Elements are everywhere: some you can see, like gold; others are almost invisible, like oxygen gas. An element is a substance that cannot be broken up into simpler ingredients. Each one is made up of tiny building blocks called atoms, which are unique for every element. Most elements are joined with other elements to make compounds, which are made by combining two or more elements. This includes water, which is a compound of hydrogen and oxygen.

Elements in our world

There are 118 elements in the periodic table; 92 of them are found in nature, while the others are made by humans. Every element is unique. Most of the elements are solids, like the metals. At room temperature, 11 elements are gases, while bromine and mercury are the only two liquids.

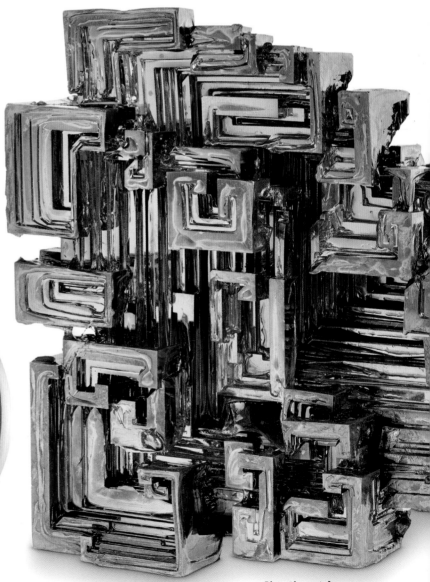

Bromine liquid with bromine gas

Bismuth crystals

Earth

Water

Air

Fire

Elements in and around us

About 99 percent of the human body is made from just six elements, though they are combined together to form thousands of different compounds. On the other hand, Earth's atmosphere is a mixture of gases, most of which are pure elements. About 99 percent of the air is made from nitrogen and oxygen.

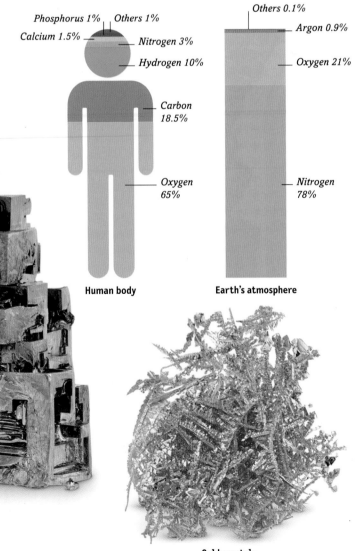

Phosphorus 1% Others 1%
Calcium 1.5%
Nitrogen 3%
Hydrogen 10%

Carbon 18.5%

Oxygen 65%

Human body

Others 0.1%
Argon 0.9%
Oxygen 21%

Nitrogen 78%

Earth's atmosphere

Gold crystals

Ancient ideas

The idea of elements is very old, dating back about 2,600 years to ancient Greece. However, Greek thinkers believed that the world was made of just four elements: earth, water, fire, and air. Empedocles, an influential scholar, was the first to propose that these elements made up all structures. Only much later did scientists learn that none of these are actually elements. For thousands of years, everybody from ancient Egyptian priests to medieval European alchemists, speculated about the definiton and classification of an element.

Iranian alchemists in their workshop

Alchemy and mysticism

Chemists are scientists who study elements and compounds. However, before they existed, the alchemists were medieval researchers. Believing in a mixture of science and magic, alchemists tried to change ordinary metals (such as lead) into gold. They failed because elements cannot be changed from one type to another. But, in the process, they discovered many new elements and developed several processes that chemists still use today.

👓 ROBERT BOYLE

The first person to use science to understand the elements was the Irish scientist and inventor Robert Boyle. He pursued science through reason, and in the 1660s he performed the first chemistry experiments to show that much of what the alchemists believed was wrong.

Inside an atom

An atom is the smallest unit of an element. Atoms are too small to see (even with the most powerful microscopes) but they are everywhere. They consist of smaller particles called protons, neutrons, and electrons. Every element has a unique number of protons.

What's the atomic number?

The number of protons in an atom of an element is called the atomic number. The atomic number of an atom identifies the element it belongs to. Every atom also has an equal number of electrons. For elements found naturally on Earth, hydrogen has the smallest atomic number (1), while uranium atoms have the highest atomic number (92).

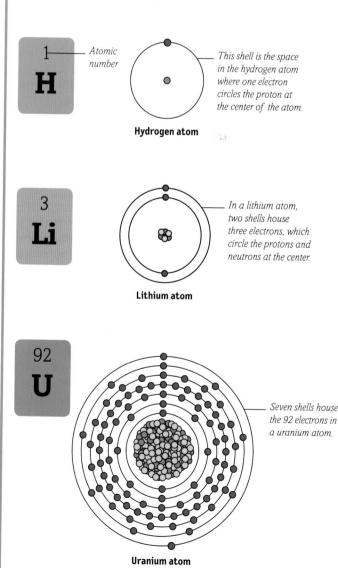

1

H

Atomic number

This shell is the space in the hydrogen atom where one electron circles the proton at the center of the atom.

Hydrogen atom

3

Li

In a lithium atom, two shells house three electrons, which circle the protons and neutrons at the center.

Lithium atom

92

U

Seven shells house the 92 electrons in a uranium atom.

Uranium atom

Electron ❭ The tiny, negatively charged particles in an atom are called electrons. They are involved in the way the atoms of an element react and form bonds with the atoms of other elements.

Shell ❭ The electrons in an atom move around the nucleus. They are arranged in layers called shells. When reacting with each other, atoms tend to fill up their outer shells to become more stable.

Neutron > As its name suggests, neutrons are neutral particles, which means they do not have an electric charge. A neutron weighs the same as a proton, and much more than a electron.

Proton > Protons have a positive electric charge. This charge attracts the negatively charged electrons, holding them in place around the nucleus. Because each proton's charge is canceled out by the equal charge of an electron, the atom has no overall charge, and is therefore neutral.

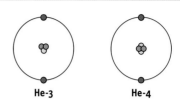

He-3   He-4

Isotopes
While every element has a unique number of electrons and protons in its atoms, the number of neutrons can vary. These different forms are called isotopes. For example, helium has two isotopes: He-3 contains one neutron, and He-4 has two neutrons.

Electromagnet attracts metal pieces

Electromagnetism
Atoms work like tiny magnets. A force called electromagnetism holds them together. It makes particles with opposite charges, such as protons and electrons, attract each other. Those with similar charges repel each other. A magnet is an object in which the magnetic forces of the atoms attract and repel other objects. An electromagnet develops magnetism when an electric current runs through it.

ATOMIC PIONEERS

During his atomic research in the early 20th century, Sir Ernest Rutherford, a New Zealand scientist, expanded our understanding of the structure of atoms. He discovered protons and proved that they were located in an atom's nucleus.

Sir Ernest Rutherford

Nucleus > The central core, or nucleus, of an atom is made up of protons and neutrons. Nearly all the mass of the atom is packed into the nucleus, and this gives every element a unique atomic mass.

Reactions and uses

Explosive reaction

In this chemical reaction, pure lithium reacts with air to make the compound lithium oxide. It takes energy to break the links between the lithium atoms and then make bonds with oxygen in the air. Reactions need energy to start, but they often produce energy as heat and light.

1. This piece of pure lithium is placed on a surface and is exposed to the air.

2. A gas torch is used to heat the lithium, and in just a few seconds it turns red, which is a typical color for this metal when it becomes hot.

3. Very quickly, the lithium catches fire. The white areas forming here are the compound lithium oxide, which is a combintion of lithium and oxygen.

The elements can combine in different ways to make 10 million compounds, possibly more. As well as learning about the physical and chemical properties of elements, chemists also want to find out how and why certain elements react with each other to form compounds. Chemical reactions are happening all the time. During a reaction, substances change into new substances. The bonds that hold them are broken and then remade in a different combination.

Mixtures

A mixture is a combination of substances that can be separated by physical means, such as filtering. It is not the same as a compound, where the ingredients are connected by bonds and can only be separated using a chemical reaction. Mixtures can be classified as solutions, colloids, and suspensions.

Solution
In this mixture, a substance is completely and evenly mixed, or dissolved, into another substance. Seawater is a solution.

Colloid
This mixture contains unevenly spread particles and clusters that are too small to see. Milk is a colloid.

Suspension
This type of mixture consists of large particles of one substance floating in another substance. Muddy water is a suspension.

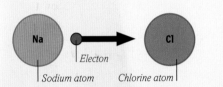

Na — Sodium atom
Electon
Cl — Chlorine atom

Na⁺ — *The sodium ion is positive.*

Cl⁻ — *The chlorine ion is negative.*

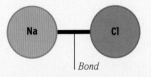

Na — **Cl**
Bond

1. A sodium atom donates one electron to a chlorine atom. This gives both atoms full outer electron shells.

2. These are now charged atoms known as ions. The sodium ion has a positive charge and the chlorine ion has a negative charge.

3. Sodium is attracted to—and forms a bond with—chlorine, forming a molecule of the compound sodium chloride.

Forming compounds

There are two kinds of bonds formed between elements during a chemical reaction. In an ionic bond, such as in sodium chloride (above), one atom gives away its electron(s) and another accepts them. This results in each having full outer electron shells. The other type is called covalent bonding. In this, atoms sit together and share their electrons so they both have full outer shells.

As lithium burns in air, it becomes lithium oxide.

Reactions in the real world

Chemical reactions happen all around us. There are reactions when we cook, take medication, or breathe. The image above shows a rusty iron ship. Over time, the element iron develops this red, flaky layer when it reacts with oxygen present in water or air to form the compound iron oxide—more commonly known as rust.

17

Pure hydrogen (H) fills this glass sphere, and produces a purple glow when electrified.

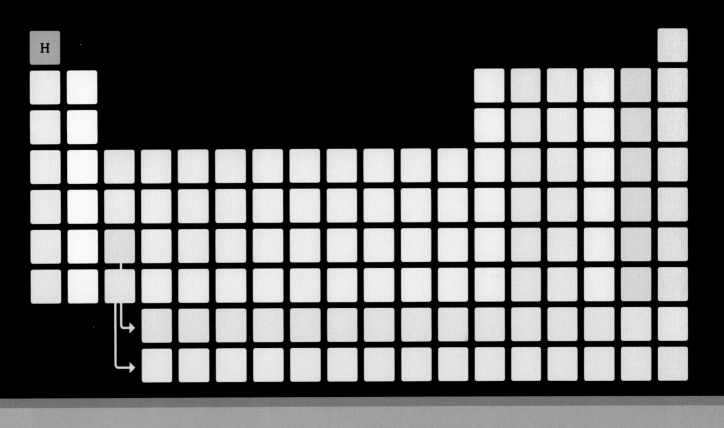

Hydrogen

The first element, hydrogen (H), is located above the alkali metals in the first column of the periodic table. However, because it is so different from the elements below it, hydrogen is not included in their group. This gas has the simplest atoms of any element, with one electron and one proton. It is highly reactive and forms compounds with all kinds of other elements.

Atomic structure
A hydrogen (H) atom has one electron moving around a nucleus consisting of a single proton.

Physical properties
Hydrogen gas is the lightest material in the universe. Pure hydrogen is rare on Earth because it escapes quickly from the atmosphere into space.

Chemical properties
Hydrogen is highly flammable. It forms compounds with both metals and nonmetals.

Compounds
The most common hydrogen compound is water. Acids are compounds that contain hydrogen.

H
1

Hydrogen

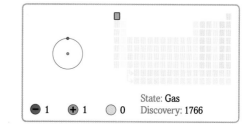

State: **Gas**
⊖ 1 ⊕ 1 ◯ 0 Discovery: 1766

Forms

Pure hydrogen in a glass sphere

Hydrogen gas is trapped inside this glass sphere, and gives off a purple glow when electrified.

The Orion Nebula

This gaseous stellar nursery is giving birth to thousands of stars.

The Sun

Jupiter

Three quarters of this planet is made up of layers of gaseous and liquid hydrogen.

The Sun *is four-fifths hydrogen.*

Water

Each water molecule has two atoms of hydrogen and one of oxygen.

Hydrogen is the first member of the periodic table because it has the simplest atoms of all elements: they contain just one proton and one electron. Pure hydrogen is a transparent gas. The biggest planets, such as **Jupiter**, are vast balls of hydrogen mixed with other gases, such as helium and methane. On Earth, hydrogen is commonly found in **water**. Although it is rare in Earth's atmosphere, hydrogen is the most common element in the universe. Stars, such as the **Sun**, contain large amounts of hydrogen. At the center of a star, atoms of

Uses

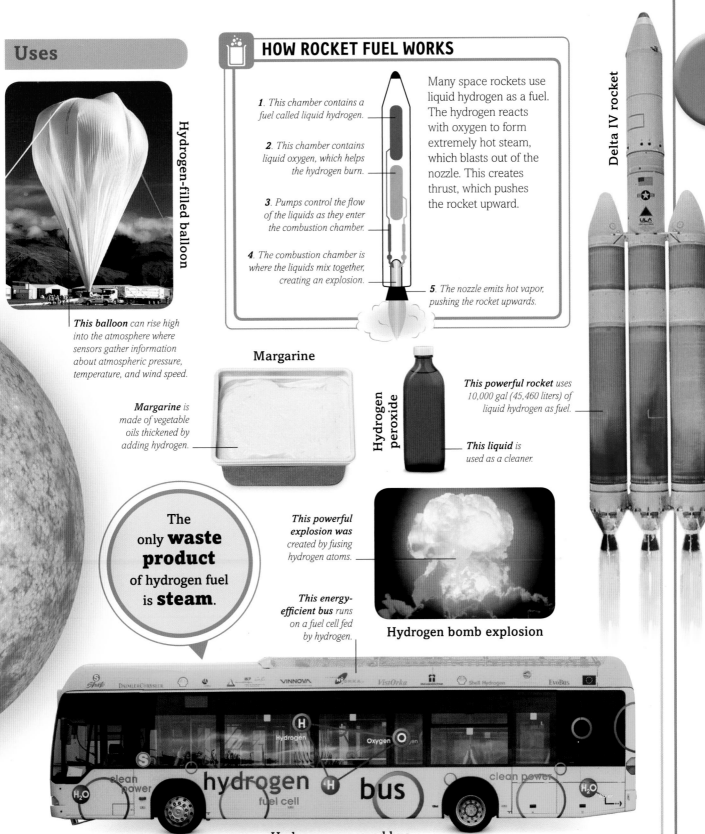

Hydrogen-filled balloon

This balloon can rise high into the atmosphere where sensors gather information about atmospheric pressure, temperature, and wind speed.

HOW ROCKET FUEL WORKS

1. This chamber contains a fuel called liquid hydrogen.

2. This chamber contains liquid oxygen, which helps the hydrogen burn.

3. Pumps control the flow of the liquids as they enter the combustion chamber.

4. The combustion chamber is where the liquids mix together, creating an explosion.

5. The nozzle emits hot vapor, pushing the rocket upwards.

Many space rockets use liquid hydrogen as a fuel. The hydrogen reacts with oxygen to form extremely hot steam, which blasts out of the nozzle. This creates thrust, which pushes the rocket upward.

Delta IV rocket

This powerful rocket uses 10,000 gal (45,460 liters) of liquid hydrogen as fuel.

Margarine

Margarine is made of vegetable oils thickened by adding hydrogen.

Hydrogen peroxide

This liquid is used as a cleaner.

The only **waste product** of hydrogen fuel is **steam**.

This powerful explosion was created by fusing hydrogen atoms.

Hydrogen bomb explosion

This energy-efficient bus runs on a fuel cell fed by hydrogen.

Hydrogen-powered bus

---

this element are fused together, releasing heat and light. New stars form inside **nebulae**—such as the **Orion Nebula**. They are clouds of hydrogen gas that slowly collapse in on themselves. Hydrogen gas is the lightest element of all, and much lighter than air. This is why **hydrogen-filled balloons** can fly higher than air-filled ones. Supercold liquid hydrogen is used as **rocket** fuel. Atoms of hydrogen fuse together to produce a lot of energy in **hydrogen bomb** explosions. Pure hydrogen is also a clean energy source used to power some **buses** and cars.

Potassium (K)
tarnishes when
exposed to air.

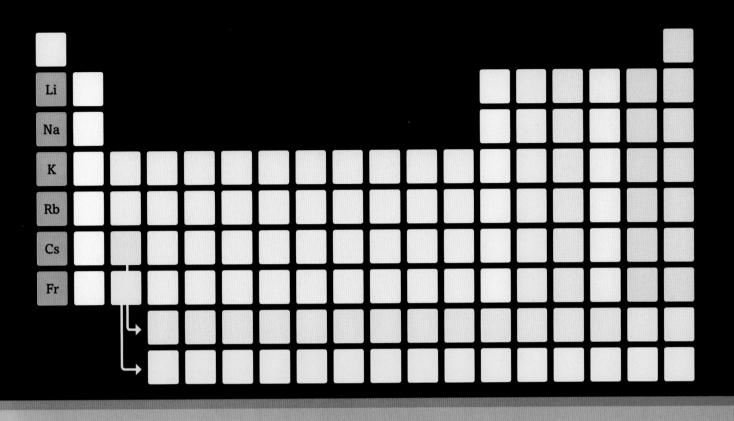

Alkali Metals

After hydrogen (H)—which is in a group of its own—the first column of the periodic table contains the alkali metals. This group gets its name from the way the elements react with water. These vigorous reactions always produce acid-attacking compounds called alkalis. None of the alkali metals are ever found in a pure form in nature. The first three metals are common in many minerals, while the last three are rarer.

Atomic structure
The atoms of all alkali metals have just one electron in their outer shell. Alkali metal atoms are among the biggest of all atoms.

Physical properties
These metals are soft enough to be cut with a knife. They are all silvery and very shiny when clean.

Chemical properties
Alkali metals are highly reactive. They form bonds with other elements, giving away their single outer electron.

Compounds
These metals react with water to form compounds called hydroxides. They react easily with halogens to form salts, such as sodium chloride.

Li Lithium

3

State: **Solid**
Discovery: 1817

● 3   ⊕ 3   ○ 4

Forms

Lepidolite

*This **water** contains tiny amounts of dissolved lithium minerals.*

Drinking water

Oyster mushrooms

These mushrooms absorb lithium from the soil.

Pale quartz

Shrimp

Shrimp and other shellfish absorb lithium from seawater.

Purple crystals containing lithium

Bar of pure lithium refined in a laboratory

Shiny pure lithium becomes dull when it is exposed to air.

Petalite

Gray-white crystals

Lithium is the the lightest of all metals: in fact, it can easily float on water. Pure lithium is very reactive and exists in nature only in minerals, such as **lepidolite** and **petalite**. Many lithium minerals dissolve well in **water**, and the world's seawater contains millions of tons of dissolved lithium. Lithium is found in many foods, such as **mushrooms**, **shrimp**, nuts, and seeds. It also has many everyday applications. Glass composed of lithium is resistant to heat and is used in scientific equipment, such as **mirrors inside**

Uses

Smartphones run on rechargeable batteries that use lithium to store electricity.

Smartphone

Hale telescope mirror

Lithium added to the glass in this mirror stops the disk warping at extreme temperatures.

LITHIUM-ION BATTERY

Lithium-ion batteries are widely used in digital devices. They store electrical energy to power gadgets and are rechargeable. This diagram shows a device's battery in use; when it is charging, this process is reversed.

3. As ions move inside the battery, negatively charged electrons are pushed through the phone, providing the electricity to make it work.

1. Inside the battery, positively charged lithium ions move from the negative electrode (-) to the positive electrode (+).

2. The positive electrode receives lithium ions as the battery loses charge.

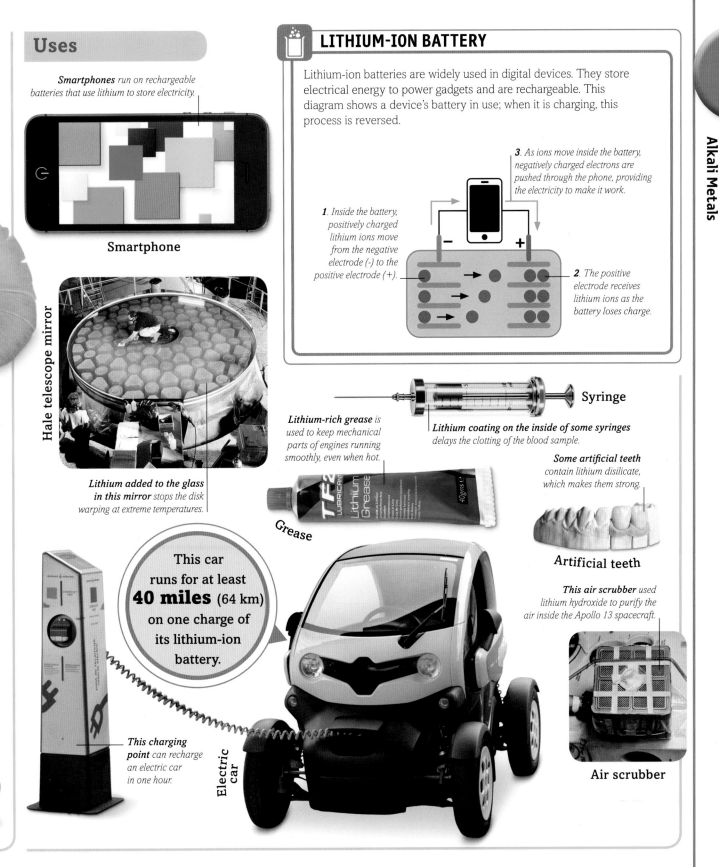

Lithium-rich grease is used to keep mechanical parts of engines running smoothly, even when hot.

Grease

Syringe

Lithium coating on the inside of some syringes delays the clotting of the blood sample.

Some artificial teeth contain lithium disilicate, which makes them strong.

Artificial teeth

This air scrubber used lithium hydroxide to purify the air inside the Apollo 13 spacecraft.

This car runs for at least **40 miles** (64 km) on one charge of its lithium-ion battery.

This charging point can recharge an electric car in one hour.

Electric car

Air scrubber

telescopes. The main use for lithium is in rechargeable batteries. Lithium-ion batteries are small but powerful, so they are ideal for **smartphones** and tablet computers. Larger lithium batteries can power **electric cars**, which are less polluting than gasoline-powered ones. A soapy compound called lithium stearate is used to make **grease**, which helps automobile engines run smoothly. This element also forms hard ceramics that are used to produce strong **artificial teeth**. Lithium compounds are used in some medicines as well.

¹¹Na Sodium

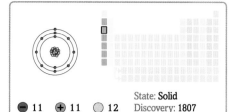

State: **Solid**
Discovery: 1807
— 11 + 11 ◯ 12

Forms

This sodium-rich mineral is an example of a zeolite, a mineral with tiny holes that can trap gases.

Clinoptilolite

Pure halite crystals

Sodalite cabochon

Soft, shiny metal

Laboratory sample of pure sodium in an airless vial

Polished gemstone made of the mineral sodalite

The thick, white crust covering this salt flat contains sodium chloride and other salts.

Cube-shaped transparent crystals

This glass case holding pure sodium has no air, which prevents the metal from reacting with oxygen in air.

Salar de Uyuni, Bolivia

Everyday salt contains lots of sodium. Although abundant on Earth, sodium is never found in its pure form naturally: it forms compounds with other elements. Sodium chloride, which also contains chlorine, is the most common sodium compound. It is also known as the mineral **halite**, and it is what makes seawater salty. Other sodium minerals include **sodalite**, a soft blue stone that can be shaped and polished. **Pure sodium** is soft enough to be cut with a knife. It reacts with oxygen in the air, forming a compound called sodium oxide, and bursts

Uses

Edible salt *is made by refining the mineral halite.*

Common salt

This mummified body, *or mummy, was preserved using sodium compounds.*

Mummy

Sodium fireworks

Bright yellow lights in fireworks *get their color from burning sodium compounds.*

Indigo dyes—*often used in blue jeans—contain sodium.*

Indigo dye powder

Spraying salt *keeps roads free from ice and frost.*

MUMMIFICATION

Ancient Egyptians believed in life after death and so preserved the bodies of their dead. A dead body was washed and the organs removed, then crystals of sodium compounds were used to dry it out. Finally, the body was wrapped, which completed the process of mummification.

1. Organs, such as the stomach and lungs, were removed from the dead body.

2. Sodium compounds were spread over the body to dry it.

3. The body was wrapped in cloth to mummify it.

This tube *glows bright yellow-orange when sodium gas is electrified.*

Sodium gas lamp

Bar of soap

Some soaps *contain sodium hydroxide.*

Baking soda

Odorless white powder

De-icing

Cats were sacred in ancient Egypt, so their bodies were mummified.

into flames when in contact with water. Sodium compounds in **fireworks** burn with a yellow-orange color. In ancient Egypt, crystals of sodium compounds were used to preserve dead bodies as **mummies**. Another useful compound is sodium bicarbonate, or **baking soda**, which makes dough rise by releasing bubbles of carbon dioxide. When refined, sodium chloride, or **common salt**, has several uses. It makes ice melt so it is used in salty grit added to slippery, frozen roads. This helps **de-ice** them to make them safer. It is also an important seasoning for meals.

SALT FLATS
Hundreds of artificial ponds dot the hillside near the small town of Maras, high in the Andes of Peru. The ponds fill with water from a stream that runs down from the nearby mountains. In the sunshine, the water evaporates, leaving behind a thick salt crust that can be collected. The people of Maras have been gathering salt in this way for at least 500 years.

The salt forms part of rocks deep underground before it is dissolved by the stream and flows into the pools. Evaporation can also be used to collect salt from seawater or other salty water sources (known as brines). Today, however, most of the world's salt comes from underground mines containing thick layers of salt that are a result of ancient seas drying out. Over millions of years, that dry salt has become buried under dense layers of rocks. This so-called "rock salt" is sometimes unearthed using excavators. At other mines, it is washed out by piping in warm water, which dissolves the salt. The brine is then pumped up to the surface for evaporation.

19 K Potassium

State: **Solid**
Discovery: **1807**
● 19 ⊕ 19 ○ 20

Forms

This mineral is rich in potassium chloride.

Potash

This glass case holding pure potassium has no air in it, preventing the metal from reacting with oxygen in air.

Laboratory sample of pure potassium in an airless vial

Soft and shiny solid

The yellow and green color comes from impurities.

This mineral contains potassium chloride, which gives it a salty taste.

Sylvite

Potassium was first found in the dust of burnt plants. It was discovered by Sir Humphry Davy when he experimented with **potash**—a mixture of substances made from the ash of burnt plants soaked in water. The name potassium comes from potash but the element's chemical symbol, K, is taken from *kalium*, a Latin word for "ash." Potassium is never found pure in nature, but is present in minerals such as **aphthitalite** and **sylvite**. Potassium is vital for the human body, helping muscles and nerves work properly. For this, we rely on

Uses

Aphthitalite

This salt contains potassium chloride, which helps lower blood pressure.

Potassium salt

Carbonated water contains potassium compounds for added flavor.

Carbonated water

Potassium solutions are used to hydrate patients.

Saline drip

Rebreather

Potassium-rich fertilizer is easily absorbed by the soil and boosts plant growth.

This cylinder contains a compound called potassium superoxide.

Gunpowder

This soap contains potassium hydroxide, which is a cleaning agent.

Liquid soap

Fertilizer

Banana

Potassium-rich food

This explosive mixture contains powdered potassium nitrate.

Avocado

Sweet potato

Toughened glass screen

This strengthened glass sheet contains potassium nitrate.

potassium-rich food, such as bananas, root vegetables, and avocados, which contain potassium chloride. In tiny amounts, this compound can enhance flavors, as it does in **carbonated water**. It is also a healthy alternative to sodium chloride, or common salt, and an important ingredient in **saline drips** for rehydrating patients who are seriously ill. Potassium nitrate is a compound of potassium, oxygen, and nitrogen, and is found in **gunpowder** and **toughened glass screens** for cell phones.

37
Rb Rubidium

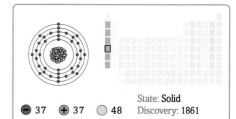

State: **Solid**
Discovery: 1861

− 37   + 37   ◯ 48

Forms

Laboratory sample of pure rubidium in an airless vial

Pale, waxy mineral

Leucite

This soft mineral contains up to 3.5% rubidium.

Lepidolite

Pollucite

Rubidium makes up only about **1 percent** of this mineral.

*This glass case contains **pure rubidium**, preventing it from coming into contact with air and catching fire.*

This ore contains cesium and rubidium.

Rubidium was named after the Latin word *rubidius,* **meaning "deepest red."** This refers to the red-colored flame it produces when burned. This highly reactive element ignites on contact with air. On contact with water, it reacts vigorously, producing hydrogen gas and a lot of heat. Rubidium is not often concentrated in particular minerals, but instead is spread in small amounts through a wide range of minerals, such as **leucite** and **pollucite**. The pure metal is sourced mainly from the mineral **lepidolite**. Another mineral called rubicline has even more

Uses

These lenses contain rubidium, which aids night vision.

Night-vision goggles

RUBIDIUM-STRONTIUM DATING

About a quarter of all rubidium atoms are radioactive. Slowly over time, they break down into strontium atoms. Comparing the amounts of these elements in a rock shows when that mineral was formed. Older rocks have less rubidium and more strontium in them.

Rubidium-87 atoms (red) decay at a predictable rate.

Only small amounts of strontium-87 (blue) in the rock.

The amount of strontium-87 has increased over time.

Millions of years ago

Present day

The structure of the brain can be seen clearly because of the use of radioactive rubidium.

This sensitive device detects light by using a rubidium compound.

Photomultiplier

Electricity cables are hung from these rubidium-rich insulators.

PET scan

931B10 Serial No.

Product **931B**

12404

Fireworks

Ceramic insulator

This purple color comes from burning a nitrogen rubidium compound.

Magnetometer

This device from the early 20th century used rubidium to measure the strength of magnetic fields.

rubidium in it but is very rare. Rubidium atoms are sensitive to light and can be used in photoelectric cells (devices that convert light energy into electricity) and **night-vision equipment**. This element has radioactive forms, which can be used to measure the age of rocks. When injected into a patient's body, rubidium targets tumors, which show up clearly on **PET (positron emission tomography) scans**. Rubidium is also used by light-sensitive electronics called **photomultipliers**, and in making **insulators** for high-voltage cables and some special types of glass.

55
Cs Cesium

State: **Solid**
− 55 + 55 ○ 78 Discovery: **1860**

Forms

The crystals of this mineral are used in jewelry.

Pollucite

Shiny, silver-gold metal

Laboratory sample of pure cesium in an airless vial

Sealed glass tube

Uses

This highly accurate clock is also called a cesium clock.

Atomic clock

High-density cesium compounds in this fluid stop toxic gases rising to the surface.

Drilling fluid

👓 KIRCHHOFF AND BUNSEN

Cesium was discovered in 1860 by German scientists Robert Bunsen and Gustav Kirchhoff. They burned a sample of mineral water on a burner, which split the flame's light into individual colors. One of them was a distinctive light blue, which came from cesium.

Gustav Kirchhoff (left) and Robert Bunsen (right)

As the most reactive metal on Earth, cesium explodes into flames if in contact with air or water. Therefore, **pure cesium**, is stored in a sealed glass tube from which all the air has been sucked out. This element is rare, and most of it is extracted from the mineral **pollucite**. Its name means "sky blue" and refers to the color of cesium's flame when burning. Cesium is used in **atomic clocks**, which measure time down to a billionth of a second. These clocks are so accurate that they would gain or lose no more than one second every 300 million years.

87 Fr Francium

State: **Solid**
— 87 + 87 ○ 136 Discovery: **1939**

Thorite

This mineral was discovered in 1828 in Norway.

👓 MARGUERITE PEREY

The French chemist Marguerite Perey discovered francium in 1939 while studying the way a pure sample of another radioactive metal—actinium—decayed. She found that actinium broke down to form thorium and a previously unknown element. She named this element francium after her home country.

The dark crust is a uranium mineral that holds tiny amounts of francium.

Earth's rocks have **one** francium **atom** for every million trillion uranium atoms.

Uraninite

Francium is one of the rarest natural elements on Earth. Scientists think there may be just 1.1 oz (30 g) of francium in Earth's rocks. Francium atoms are created when radioactive elements break down. Francium can be extracted from radioactive ores such as **thorite** and **uraninite**, both of which contain tiny amounts of this element. Even so, to date the largest sample of the metal made contained only 300,000 atoms, and lasted only a few days. Francium has no known uses outside of research.

Barium (Ba) crystals turn black in the air.

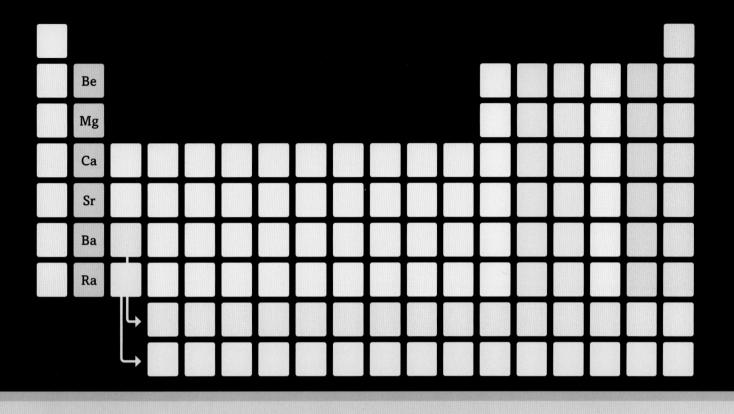

Alkaline Earth Metals

This group is a collection of reactive metals that were discovered as compounds inside common minerals in Earth's crust. Most of these minerals—known in the past as "earths"—are alkaline (alkali-producing), and this is how the group got its name. All alkaline earth metals were first purified in the 19th century.

Atomic structure
The alkaline earth metals have two electrons in their outermost electron shell. Radium (Ra) is the most radioactive member.

Physical properties
All members of this group are soft and shiny when pure. They are solid at room temperature.

Chemical properties
These metals are similar to the alkali metals, but not as reactive. Except for beryllium (Be), all alkaline earth metals react with hot water or steam.

Compounds
These elements form compounds with nonmetals by losing their outermost electrons. Several compounds are found in teeth and bones.

4 Be Beryllium

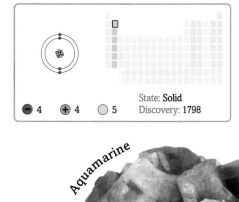

State: **Solid**
Discovery: 1798

⊖ 4   ⊕ 4   ◯ 5

Forms

This mineral can also be brown, green, or orange.

Aquamarine

These crystals have this pale blue color due to iron impurities.

Chrysoberyl

Laboratory sample of pure beryllium

Beryllium is found in more than **30 kinds of mineral**.

Lightweight metal

This widely used element gets its name from the Greek word *beryllos*, after which the mineral beryl is also named. Beryllium is the lightest of the alkaline earth metals, but it does not share many of the group's properties. For example, it does not react with water and is much harder than the other metals in its group. Two common beryllium minerals are **chrysoberyl** and beryl. Beryl has different forms, such as **aquamarine** and emerald. Beryllium is useful in many ways. For example, some military **helicopters** use windows made

38

Uses

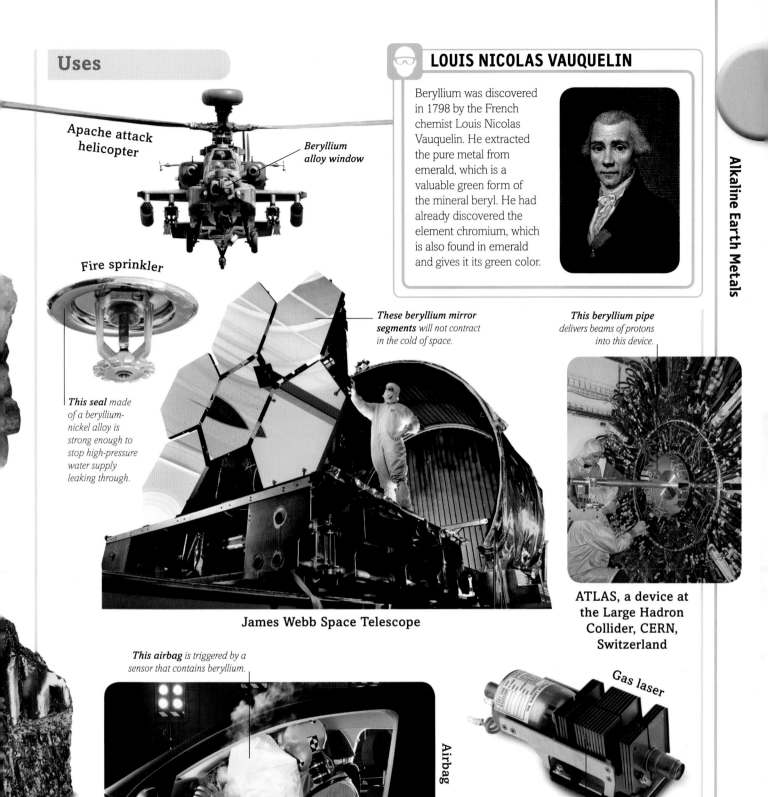

Apache attack helicopter

Beryllium alloy window

Fire sprinkler

This seal made of a beryllium-nickel alloy is strong enough to stop high-pressure water supply leaking through.

LOUIS NICOLAS VAUQUELIN

Beryllium was discovered in 1798 by the French chemist Louis Nicolas Vauquelin. He extracted the pure metal from emerald, which is a valuable green form of the mineral beryl. He had already discovered the element chromium, which is also found in emerald and gives it its green color.

These beryllium mirror segments will not contract in the cold of space.

This beryllium pipe delivers beams of protons into this device.

James Webb Space Telescope

ATLAS, a device at the Large Hadron Collider, CERN, Switzerland

This airbag is triggered by a sensor that contains beryllium.

Airbag

Gas laser

The heat sinks of this argon gas laser are made of **beryllium oxide**, which quickly conducts heat away from the laser.

of beryllium-rich glass to shield optical sensors to aid pilots flying at night or through fog. Objects made of this metal keep their shape well and hardly expand or contract if the temperature changes. This makes beryllium useful in valves for **fire sprinklers** and car sensors that trigger **airbags**. NASA's **James Webb Space Telescope** will use a large beryllium mirror that is light and strong. Beryllium oxide is made into a ceramic and used in lasers and microwave generators. Alloys of beryllium and copper are used in springs as well.

12 Mg Magnesium

State: **Solid**
Discovery: 1755

− 12   ⊕ 12   ○ 12

Alkaline Earth Metals

Forms

This green, magnesium-rich mineral forms deep underground.

Serpentine

Featherlike appearance

Tremolite

Shiny, gray crystallized form

Laboratory sample of pure magnesium

Magnesium has **22 known isotopes**.

Dolomite

This ore is a natural form of magnesium carbonate.

Magnesium was named after Magnesia in Greece. This element largely exists deep inside Earth's mantle, but it can also be found in seawater and many minerals in our planet's crust, including **serpentine**. Another mineral, **dolomite**, is also a source of **pure magnesium**.

Magnesium has many important applications. Alloys of magnesium are not only strong, but also lightweight, so are used in a range of objects, from **car wheels** to **cameras**. For centuries, many naturally occurring magnesium minerals have been used in traditional medicines.

40

Uses

Alloy wheel

Magnesium alloy makes this wheel strong and shiny.

MAGNESIUM IN CHLOROPHYLL

Chlorophyll is an important molecule in plants and is what makes them green. At its center sits a magnesium atom, which helps plants convert sunlight into energy in a process called photosynthesis.

Chlorophyll molecule

The magnesium alloy body of this camera is lightweight and will not rust.

Digital camera

Epsom salts

Crystals containing magnesium sulfate are added to warm water for a soothing bath.

Talcum powder makes skin smooth and soft.

Talcum powder

White lights from burning magnesium compounds

This indigestion medicine is a mixture of water and magnesium carbonate.

Magnesium fireworks

Milk of magnesia

Portland cement

This widely used cement contains powdered magnesium oxide.

The magnesium alloy case of this laptop is strong but lightweight.

Laptop

Magnesium carbonate, or **magnesia**, reacts with acid in the stomach to settle indigestion. Heating magnesia produces magnesium oxide, which is one of the ingredients in **cement**. Magnesium compounds are also used in **fireworks**, and they burn hot with a white flame. Salts composed of magnesium, called **Epsom salts**, named after the place in England where they were first mined, work as a muscle relaxant. Magnesium silicate, known as **talc**, is a soft mineral used in body powders.

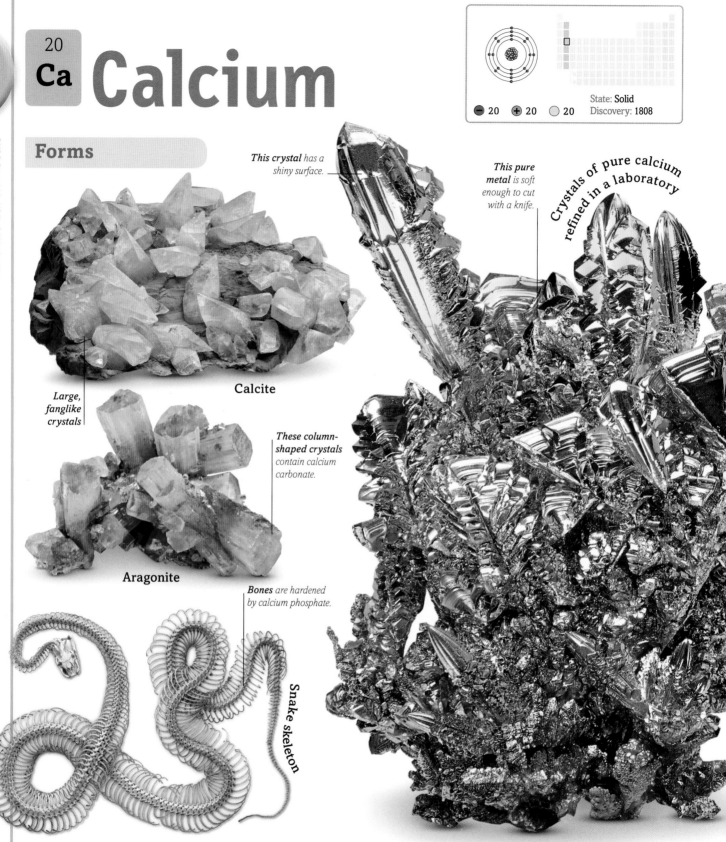

20 Ca Calcium

State: **Solid**
Discovery: 1808

● 20 ⊕ 20 ○ 20

Forms

This crystal has a shiny surface.

This pure metal is soft enough to cut with a knife.

Crystals of pure calcium refined in a laboratory

Calcite

Large, fanglike crystals

These column-shaped crystals contain calcium carbonate.

Aragonite

Bones are hardened by calcium phosphate.

Snake skeleton

The most abundant metal in the human body, calcium is also the fifth most common element on Earth. It appears in many minerals: **calcite** and **aragonite** are made of a compound of calcium and carbon called calcium carbonate. Bones in animal **skeletons** contain the compound calcium phosphate. The hard, outer layers of many other animals, such as the **shells** of sea snails, are made of calcium carbonate. Calcium is very important in our diet. We get calcium by eating **calcium-rich food**, including dairy products, green

42

Uses

This tablet contains calcium carbonate, which is an alkali—a substance that balances out acids.

Antacid tablets

Sea shell

Shells of sea snails are hardened by calcium carbonate absorbed from sea water.

An adult **human** contains about **2 lb (1 kg) of calcium** in the body.

CALCIUM CAVES

As running water flows into caves, it deposits calcium carbonate. These deposits build up to form structures called stalactites and stalagmites.

Water with dissolved calcium carbonate flows through a crack and into the cave.

Stalactite hangs from the ceiling.

Stalagmite grows up from the ground.

Water drips onto the ground.

Over time, calcium carbonate starts to build up on the ground and ceiling.

Plaster cast

This plaster of Paris cast hardens when dry, supporting broken bones.

Writing chalk

These chalks contain calcium sulfate.

Calcium-rich food

Milk

Marble forms when limestone comes under high temperature and pressure.

Marble statue

The Sphinx, Egypt

Broccoli

Orange

This statue is made of limestone, a natural rock containing calcium carbonate.

vegetables, and nuts. Oranges are also a good source of calcium, and most orange juices have extra calcium added to them. **Antacid tablets**, used to settle indigestion, contain calcium carbonate. This compound reacts with acid in the stomach. Calcium compounds are also common in construction materials. Plasterboard, which is used to make walls smooth, **writing chalk**, and **Plaster of Paris** are all made from the mineral gypsum. Calcium oxide is an important ingredient in cement and helps turn it into hard concrete.

FLY GEYSER
The multicolored Fly Geyser in the Black Rock Desert of Nevada is made from a mound of calcium carbonate rock. Such mounds and pools are made naturally in many other places where springs gush out warm, calcium-rich waters. The amazing colors of the rocks are caused by algae and bacteria that live in this water.

Fly Geyser is not a natural wonder. It was made by accident in 1964 when engineers were drilling a well to find a source of hot water. They did find a small reservoir of water that is heated by volcanic activity deep beneath the surface, but they chose to cap the well and look elsewhere. Eventually, the hot water broke through, creating a natural fountain, or geyser. Over the decades, the calcium deposits have slowly built up. The central mound is now 5 ft (1.5 m) tall and nearly 13 ft (4 m) wide. The scalding water that gushes out can reach a height of 5 ft (1.5 m).

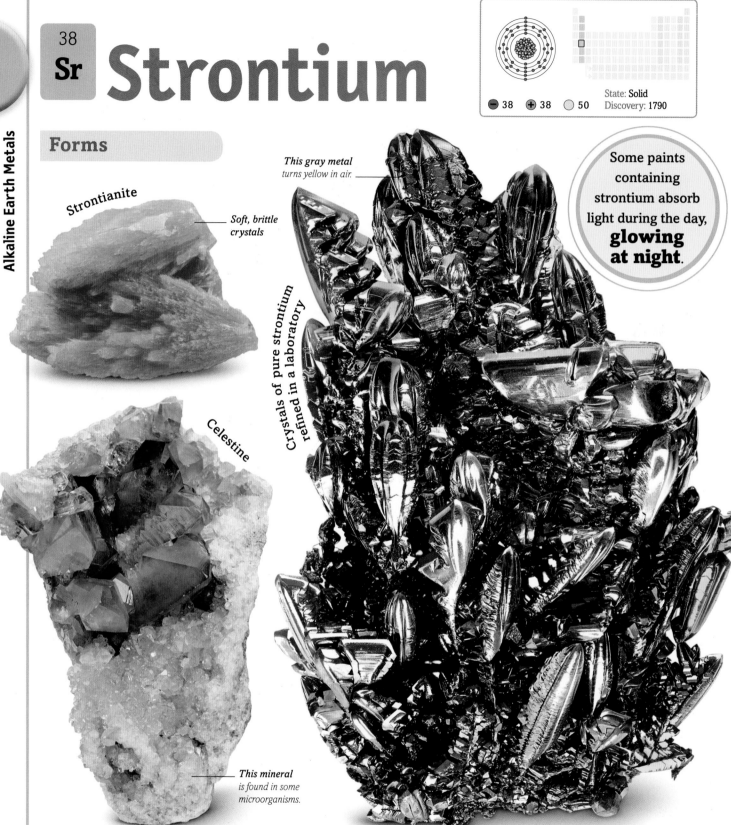

38
Sr Strontium

State: Solid
Discovery: 1790

− 38   + 38   ○ 50

Forms

Strontianite

Soft, brittle crystals

Celestine

This gray metal turns yellow in air.

Crystals of pure strontium refined in a laboratory

Some paints containing strontium absorb light during the day, **glowing at night**.

This mineral is found in some microorganisms.

Strontium was discovered in 1790 in a mineral found near the Scottish village of Strontian. The mineral burned with a bright crimson flame, and Scottish chemist Thomas Charles Hope studied it and found that it contained a new element. This mineral was called **strontianite**, and it is the main ore of strontium. **Pure strontium** was first extracted by British chemist Humphry Davy in 1808, who conducted an experiment using electricity to obtain the element from the mineral. Strontium was once used in television screens, but today

Uses

Glazed ceramic

The bowl's smooth finish is due to strontium oxide.

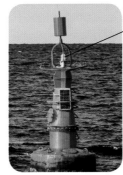

Lights in unmanned buoys can be powered by radioactive strontium.

Navigation buoy

Loudspeaker

Strontium burns in air with a bright red color.

Flare

Strontium compounds in some toothpastes provide relief from pain.

Magnets inside this loudspeaker contain strontium.

Toothpaste for sensitive teeth

Unmanned radar stations run on electricity produced using a form of strontium called strontium-90.

GENERATING ELECTRICITY

A radioactive form of strontium, called an isotope, can be used to produce electricity. A radioisotopic thermoelectrical generator (RTG) converts heat from the element into electricity for use in spacecraft.

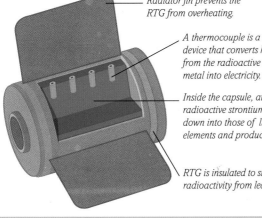

Radiator fin prevents the RTG from overheating.

A thermocouple is a device that converts heat from the radioactive metal into electricity.

Inside the capsule, atoms of radioactive strontium break down into those of lighter elements and produce heat.

RTG is insulated to stop radioactivity from leaking out.

Weather radar station

there are fewer uses for it. Strontium oxide in pottery and **ceramic** glazes creates distinctive colors, while strontium carbonate produces a red color in **flares** and fireworks. Magnets that contain iron oxide can be made stronger by adding strontium to them. These strong magnets are used in **loudspeakers** and microwave ovens. Strontium chloride is added to some kinds of **toothpaste**, while radioactive strontium is a source of electricity for **radar stations** in remote places where there are no power lines or fuel supplies.

56
Ba Barium

State: **Solid**
Discovery: 1808

⊖ 56   ⊕ 56   ◯ 81

Forms

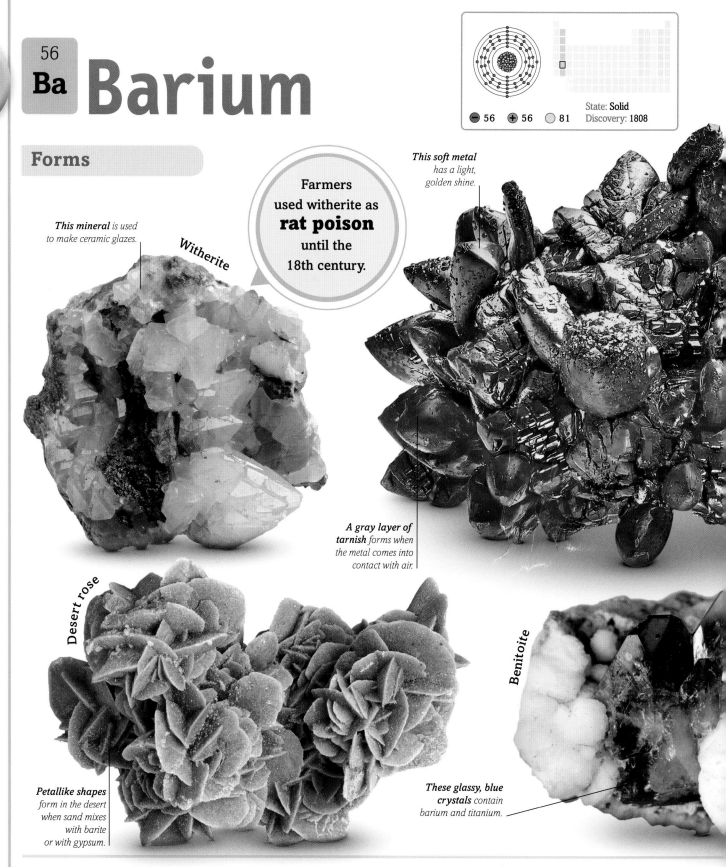

This mineral is used to make ceramic glazes.

Witherite

Farmers used witherite as **rat poison** until the 18th century.

This soft metal has a light, golden shine.

A gray layer of tarnish forms when the metal comes into contact with air.

Desert rose

Petallike shapes form in the desert when sand mixes with barite or with gypsum.

Benitoite

These glassy, blue crystals contain barium and titanium.

Barium is named after the Greek word *barys*, which means "heavy," because barium and its minerals are dense. The **pure form** of this element was first discovered in 1808 by the English chemist Humphry Davy, who extracted it from an oxide of barium. This does not exist in nature. Davy obtained it by heating the mineral **witherite**. Today, the main source of barium is barite, a mineral of sulfur that forms in deserts and in rock deposits that come into contact with hot water. A rarer mineral called **benitoite** also contains barium. The

Uses

Spark plug

This plug contains an alloy of barium and nickel.

Laboratory sample of pure barium crystals

Glass-making

This glass can be made shinier by adding barium oxide and barium carbonate.

BARIUM SOLUTION

Barium is used in a medical test for checking a patient's digestive tract for problems. In this test, a patient swallows a barium liquid solution, which fills the organs in the digestive tract.

1. The barium solution is ingested.

2. The solution enters the stomach and begins to fill it.

3. Under an X-ray scan, the barium-filled stomach shows up clearly.

This pot is made from clay that is rich in barium.

Jasperware pot

The barium in the metallic strip absorbs gases in the tube, maintaining a vacuum.

Vacuum tube

The intestine is filled with a barium solution.

X-ray scan

element is used in **spark plugs** to make them produce more powerful sparks and is added to **glass** to increase its shine. Barium compounds are added to some types of clay used for making **pots** and vases. In oil wells, barium compounds are added to drilling fluids to increase their density. Doctors make use of barium's density by giving patients a solution of barium compound to swallow before taking **X-rays** of their digestive system. The barium makes the soft digestive organs denser, allowing them to be seen clearly with an X-ray machine.

88
Ra Radium

State: **Solid**
Discovery: 1898
● 88 ⊕ 88 ○ 138

Forms

Chunk of uraninite

This ore contains just 0.02 oz (0.7 g) of radium in every 2,205 lb (1,000 kg) of rock.

In **100 years'** time, only 4% of the radium atoms in this watch would have broken down.

Radium is the only radioactive member of the alkaline earth metals. It is also the rarest element in this group, and forms in small amounts when the atoms of more common metals—such as uranium and thorium—break down. Radium atoms do not survive for long, with most of them quickly decaying into radon, a radioactive noble gas. This element is highly dangerous and is rarely used today. However, in the early 20th century, radium compounds were in common use. Luminous paints, like those used to make **watch dials**

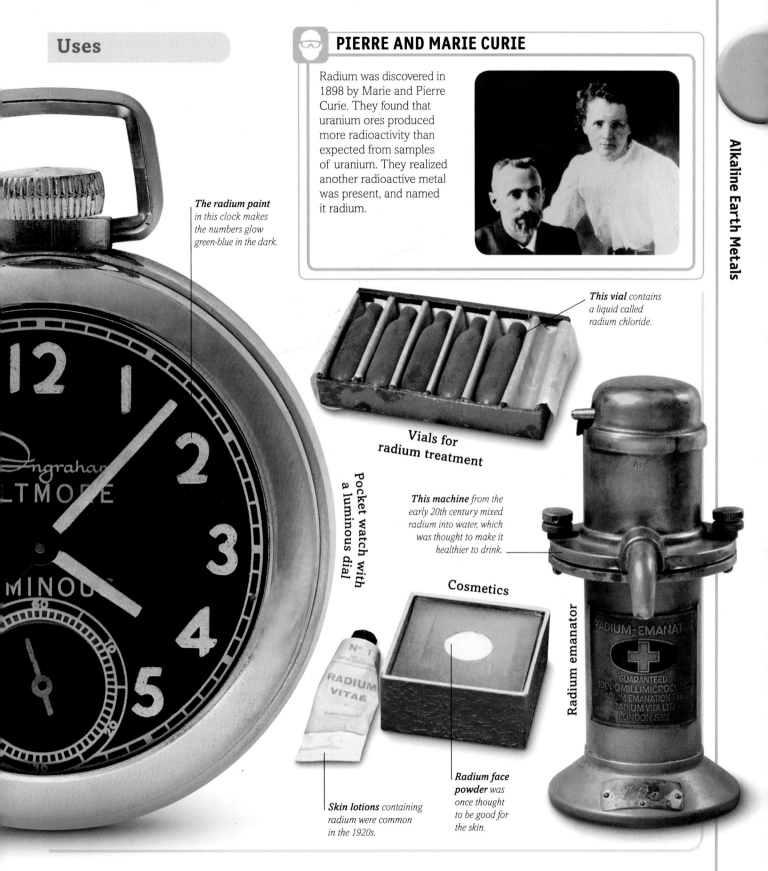

PIERRE AND MARIE CURIE

Radium was discovered in 1898 by Marie and Pierre Curie. They found that uranium ores produced more radioactivity than expected from samples of uranium. They realized another radioactive metal was present, and named it radium.

The radium paint in this clock makes the numbers glow green-blue in the dark.

This vial contains a liquid called radium chloride.

Vials for radium treatment

Pocket watch with a luminous dial

This machine from the early 20th century mixed radium into water, which was thought to make it healthier to drink.

Cosmetics

Radium emanator

RADIUM-EMANATOR

GUARANTEED
10000 MILLIMICROCURIE
OF RADIUM-EMANATION PER DAY
RADIUM VITA LTD
LONDON S.W.

Skin lotions containing radium were common in the 1920s.

Radium face powder was once thought to be good for the skin.

glow in the dark, were created using radium. People working with this paint often became ill, especially with cancer, because the radiation produced by radium damages DNA. Nevertheless, until the 1940s, many people thought radium's radioactivity made them stronger, not weaker. They injected themselves with **vials containing a radium compound**, believing it gave them an energy boost. They also thought creams and **cosmetics** with radium in them made the skin healthier, even though they did exactly the opposite.

Oddly shaped piece of pure cobalt (Co).

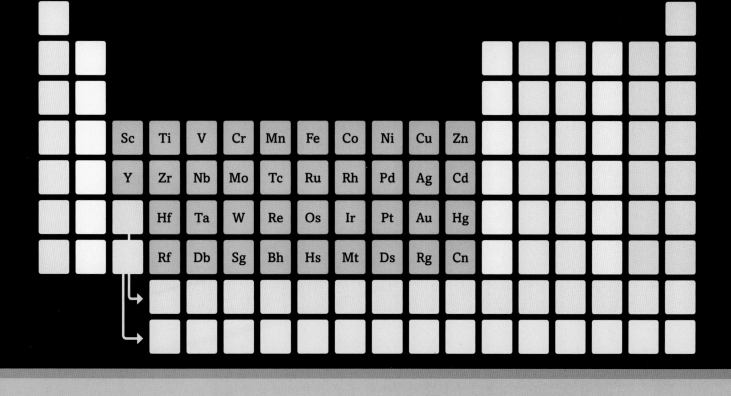

		Sc	Ti	V	Cr	Mn	Fe	Co	Ni	Cu	Zn						
		Y	Zr	Nb	Mo	Tc	Ru	Rh	Pd	Ag	Cd						
		Hf	Ta	W	Re	Os	Ir	Pt	Au	Hg							
		Rf	Db	Sg	Bh	Hs	Mt	Ds	Rg	Cn							

Transition Metals

This is the largest set of elements in the periodic table. This block of metals contains useful elements, such as gold (Au), iron (Fe), and copper (Cu). Many of these metals are easy to shape. The fourth period of the block—from rutherfordium (Rf) to copernicium (Cn)—are artificial and do not occur in nature. They were created by scientists in laboratories.

Atomic structure
Most transition metals have two outer electrons, but a few, such as copper (Cu), have just one.

Physical properties
These elements are generally hard and dense metals. Mercury (Hg), the only element that is liquid at room temperature, also belongs to this group.

Chemical properties
Transition metals are not as reactive as alkali and alkaline earth metals. However, they form many varied and colorful compounds.

Compounds
Many compounds of transition metals are brightly colored. These metals are often used in alloys, such as brass and steel.

21 Sc Scandium

State: **Solid**
Discovery: 1879

− 21 + 21 ◯ 24

Forms

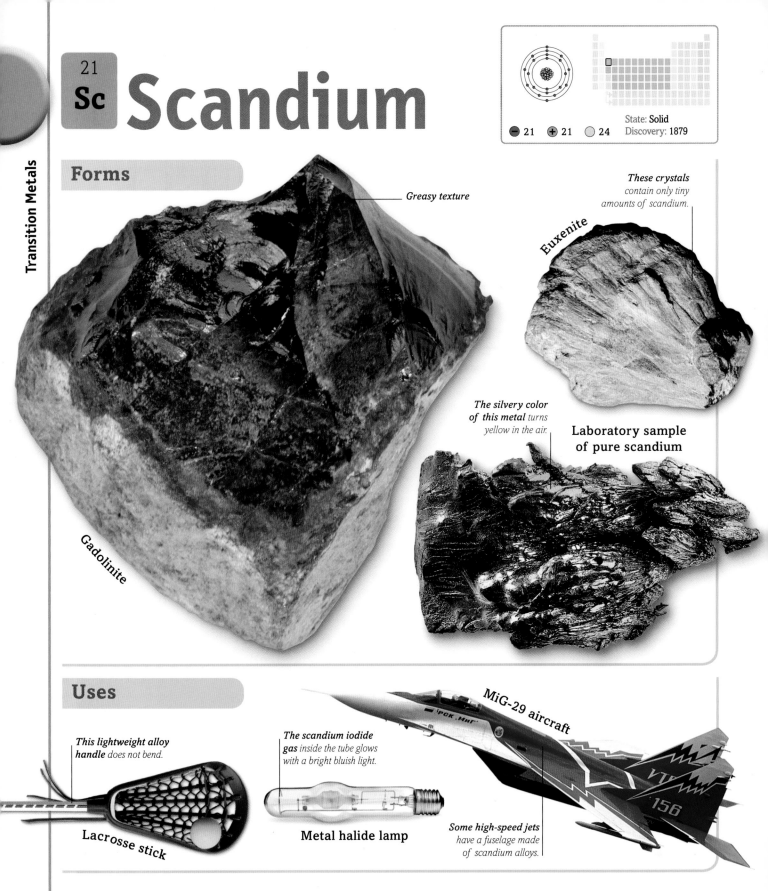

Greasy texture

These crystals contain only tiny amounts of scandium.

Euxenite

The silvery color of this metal turns yellow in the air.

Laboratory sample of pure scandium

Gadolinite

Uses

This lightweight alloy handle does not bend.

Lacrosse stick

The scandium iodide gas inside the tube glows with a bright bluish light.

Metal halide lamp

MiG-29 aircraft

Some high-speed jets have a fuselage made of scandium alloys.

156

A soft and lightweight metal, scandium is similar to aluminum. It is spread so thinly in Earth's rocks that it is very difficult to collect a large amount of this element. Scandium is only used for specialized applications. Its main ores are the minerals **gadolinite** and **euxenite**, which also contain small amounts of many other rare metals, such as cerium and yttrium. Scandium mixed with aluminum makes a strong alloy, which is used in lightweight equipment for sports, such as **lacrosse**, and to make high-speed jets, such as the **MiG-29**.

22 Ti Titanium

State: **Solid**
Discovery: 1791

- 22 + 22 ○ 26

Forms

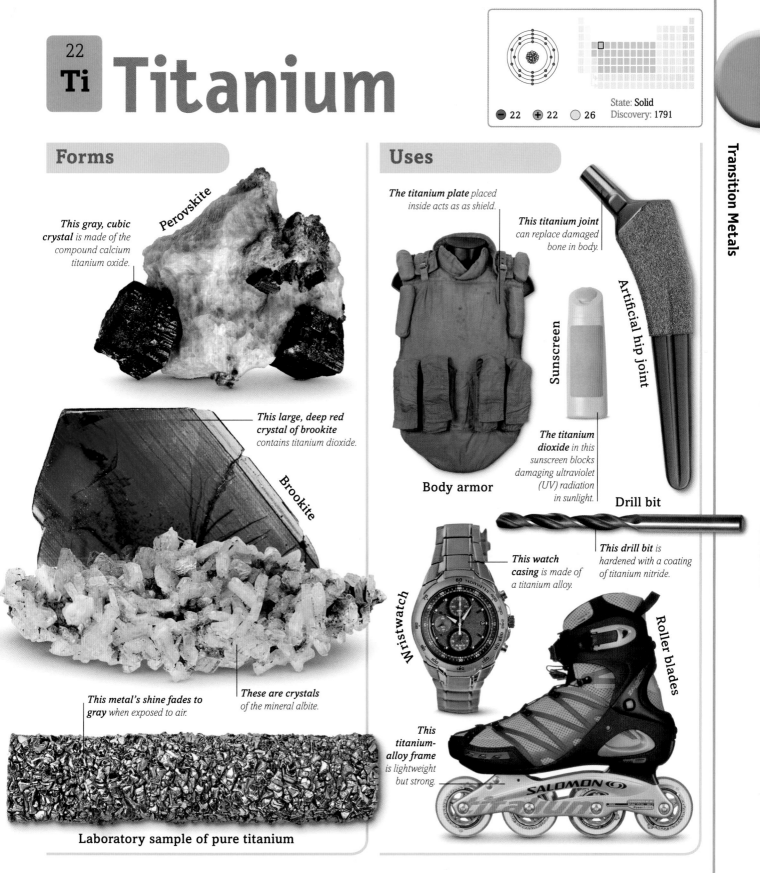

Perovskite

This gray, cubic crystal is made of the compound calcium titanium oxide.

This large, deep red crystal of brookite contains titanium dioxide.

Brookite

These are crystals of the mineral albite.

This metal's shine fades to gray when exposed to air.

Laboratory sample of pure titanium

Uses

The titanium plate placed inside acts as as shield.

This titanium joint can replace damaged bone in body.

Artificial hip joint

Sunscreen

The titanium dioxide in this sunscreen blocks damaging ultraviolet (UV) radiation in sunlight.

Body armor

This watch casing is made of a titanium alloy.

Wristwatch

This drill bit is hardened with a coating of titanium nitride.

Drill bit

Roller blades

This titanium-alloy frame is lightweight but strong.

Named after the Titans, a race of mythic Greek gods, titanium is a silvery metal. It is as strong as steel but much lighter, and it is not corroded by water or chemicals. This strong metal also makes excellent protective shields in **body armor**. Titanium is commonly used to prepare titanium dioxide, a compound of titanium and oxygen that is used in paints and **sunscreen**. Titanium is not toxic so it can be used to make medical implants, such as artificial **hip joints**. **Wristwatches** made with titanium alloys are light and strong.

23
V Vanadium

State: **Solid**
Discovery: 1801

– 23   + 23   ○ 28

Forms

Vanadinite

This mushroom contains high levels of vanadium.

Fly agaric mushroom

Carnotite

Silvery surface

This powdery yellow crust contains tiny amounts of vanadium.

These brittle crystals are the main source of vanadium.

Laboratory sample of pure vanadium crystals

Uses

Spanners

Tools made with alloys of vanadium and steel are durable.

About **85% of all vanadium** is used to toughen steel.

This knife has been strengthened by the addition of vanadium.

Damascus Steel knife

Vanadium can be hammered and stretched without breaking. This hard, strong metal is easy to shape. **Vanadium** was first **purified** in 1869 by the British chemist Henry Roscoe. Today, it is commonly extracted from its ore **vanadinite**. Ancient metalworkers used tiny amounts of vanadium compounds to make a very tough substance called **Damascus Steel**. This was named after the capital city of Syria, where ironworkers made the world's sharpest swords. Vanadium is still used to toughen tools, such as **spanners** and knives.

24 Cr Chromium

State: **Solid**
24 + 24 28 Discovery: 1798

Forms

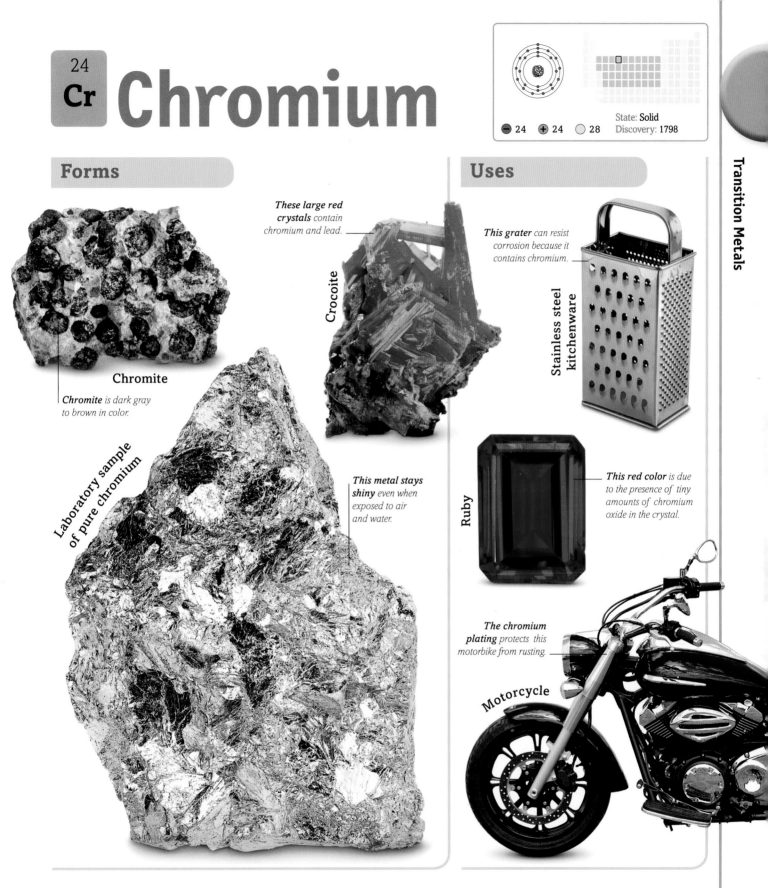

These large red crystals contain chromium and lead.

Crocoite

Chromite

Chromite is dark gray to brown in color.

Laboratory sample of pure chromium

This metal stays shiny even when exposed to air and water.

Uses

This grater can resist corrosion because it contains chromium.

Stainless steel kitchenware

Ruby

This red color is due to the presence of tiny amounts of chromium oxide in the crystal.

The chromium plating protects this motorbike from rusting.

Motorcycle

Chromium is named after *chroma,* **the Greek word for "color."** Many minerals of chromium, including **chromite** and **crocoite,** are brightly colored. An artificial form of crocoite, known as "chrome yellow," was once used in paints, but it was banned when scientists discovered it to be poisonous. **Pure chromium** doesn't corrode easily, so it is combined with iron and carbon to produce **stainless steel.** Chromium also gives gemstones, such as **rubies,** their deep-red color. Some **motorcycles** have chromium-plated bodywork, giving them a shiny finish.

25 Mn Manganese

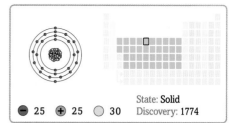

State: **Solid**

⊖ 25 ⊕ 25 ◯ 30

Discovery: 1774

Forms

Transparent, rose-colored crystal

Rhodochrosite

Shiny, silvery metal

Manganese was **purified** from **pyrolusite** for the first time in 1774.

Pyrolusite

This mineral is made of manganese dioxide.

Like magnesium, this element gets its name from the Greek region of Magnesia. There are many manganese minerals, including the colorful mineral **rhodochrosite**. The pure form of the metal is obtained mainly from the ore **pyrolusite**. **Pure manganese** is dense, hard, and brittle. This element is present in seawater as the compounds manganese hydroxide and manganese oxide, which have built up in layers over millions of years to form masses on the seabed. The human body needs a tiny amount of manganese, which we can get

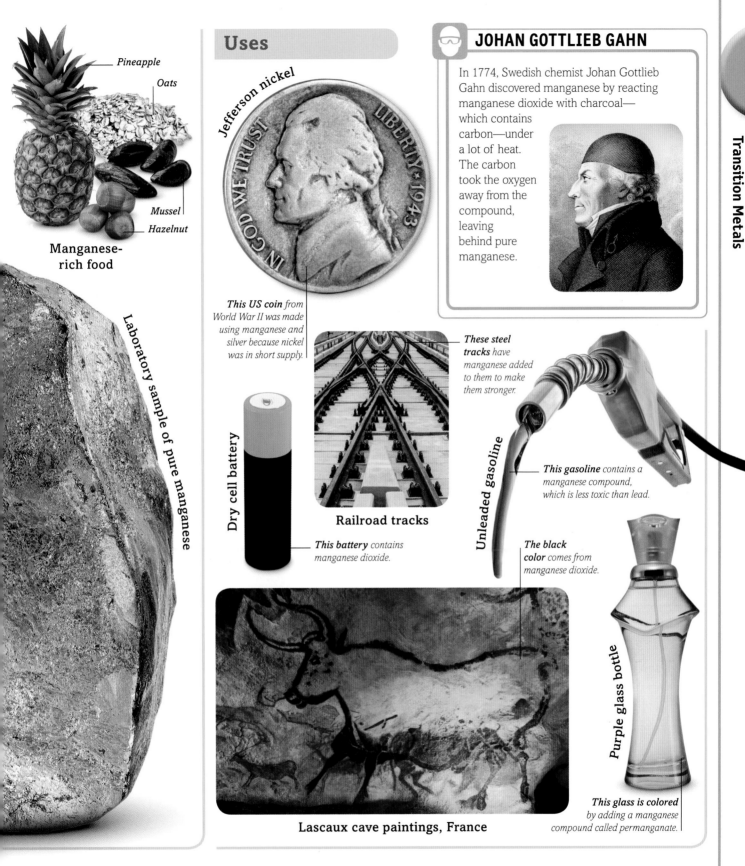

Pineapple

Oats

Mussel

Hazelnut

Manganese-rich food

Laboratory sample of pure manganese

Uses

Jefferson nickel

This US coin *from World War II was made using manganese and silver because nickel was in short supply.*

JOHAN GOTTLIEB GAHN

In 1774, Swedish chemist Johan Gottlieb Gahn discovered manganese by reacting manganese dioxide with charcoal—which contains carbon—under a lot of heat. The carbon took the oxygen away from the compound, leaving behind pure manganese.

These steel tracks *have manganese added to them to make them stronger.*

Dry cell battery

Railroad tracks

This battery *contains manganese dioxide.*

Unleaded gasoline

This gasoline *contains a manganese compound, which is less toxic than lead.*

The black color *comes from manganese dioxide.*

Purple glass bottle

Lascaux cave paintings, France

This glass is colored *by adding a manganese compound called permanganate.*

from mussels, nuts, oats, and pineapple. The applications of manganese include its use in strengthening steel, which is used in making **railroad tracks** and tank armor. Certain **dry cell batteries** carry a mixture containing manganese oxide. Manganese compounds are also added to **gasoline** and used to clean impurities from **glass** to make it clear or to give it a purple color. In prehistoric times, the compound manganese dioxide was crushed to make the dark colors used in **cave paintings**.

26
Fe Iron

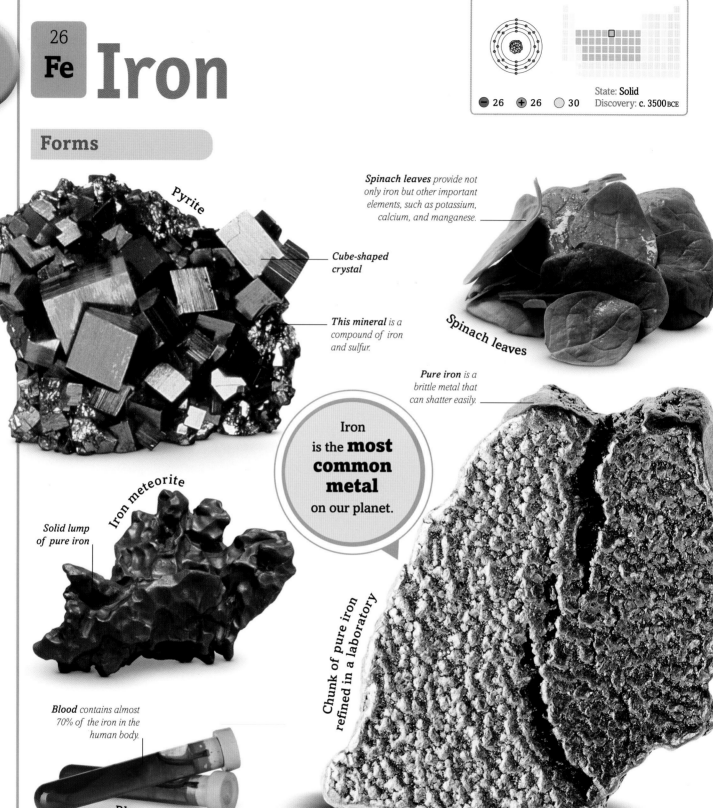

State: **Solid**
● 26 ⊕ 26 ○ 30   Discovery: **c. 3500** BCE

Forms

Pyrite

Spinach leaves *provide not only iron but other important elements, such as potassium, calcium, and manganese.*

Spinach leaves

Cube-shaped crystal

This mineral *is a compound of iron and sulfur.*

Pure iron *is a brittle metal that can shatter easily.*

Iron is the **most common metal** on our planet.

Iron meteorite

Solid lump of pure iron

Chunk of pure iron refined in a laboratory

Blood *contains almost 70% of the iron in the human body.*

Blood sample

Most of the iron on our planet is locked away in Earth's hot, molten core. This element is widely found in rocks worldwide, and almost 2.75 billion tons (2.5 billion metric tons) of iron is purified every year. Mineral ores rich in iron include **pyrite**. Other ores, including hematite, are used to extract **pure iron** in a process called smelting. **Iron-rich meteorites**—chunks of rock from outer space that crash to Earth—are one of very few sources of naturally pure iron. The human body uses iron to make hemoglobin, a substance in blood that carries oxygen around our body (oxygen

Uses

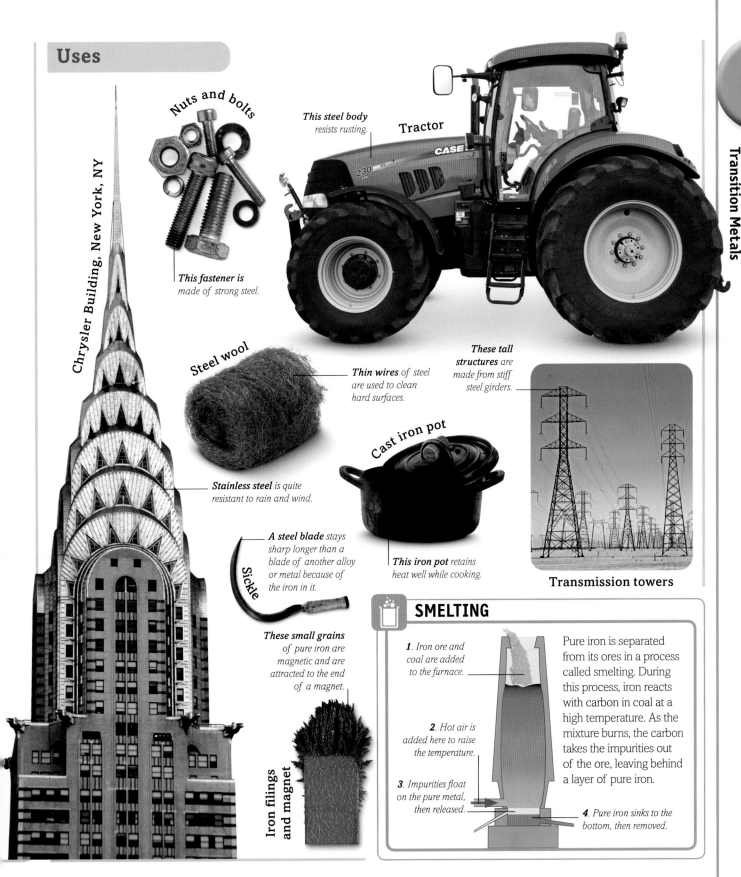

Chrysler Building, New York, NY

Nuts and bolts

This fastener is made of strong steel.

This steel body resists rusting.

Tractor

CASE 230

Steel wool

Thin wires of steel are used to clean hard surfaces.

These tall structures are made from stiff steel girders.

Stainless steel is quite resistant to rain and wind.

Cast iron pot

This iron pot retains heat well while cooking.

A steel blade stays sharp longer than a blade of another alloy or metal because of the iron in it.

Sickle

Transmission towers

These small grains of pure iron are magnetic and are attracted to the end of a magnet.

Iron filings and magnet

SMELTING

1. Iron ore and coal are added to the furnace.

2. Hot air is added here to raise the temperature.

3. Impurities float on the pure metal, then released.

4. Pure iron sinks to the bottom, then removed.

Pure iron is separated from its ores in a process called smelting. During this process, iron reacts with carbon in coal at a high temperature. As the mixture burns, the carbon takes the impurities out of the ore, leaving behind a layer of pure iron.

helps our cells produce energy for the body to work). Foods containing iron include meats and green vegetables, such as **spinach**. When pure iron comes into contact with air and water, it develops a flaky, reddish-brown coating called rust, which weakens the metal. In order to make iron tougher, tiny amounts of carbon and other metals, such as nickel and titanium, are added to it. This forms an alloy called steel, which is used to make **bolts** and strong **tractor** bodies, among other applications. Adding the element chromium to steel creates a stronger alloy called stainless steel.

STEELMAKING
A stream of hot, white liquid metal pours from a furnace at a steelmaking workshop. This is the end of a long process in which iron ore is transformed into steel, a tough alloy that is strong enough to make girders for supporting skyscrapers and bridges. The steel may even be molded into car bodies, woven into superstrong cables for elevators, or turned into powerful magnets that can levitate maglev trains.

Steel is an alloy of iron that contains about two percent carbon and some other elements. The carbon locks all the atoms together and prevents the metal from bending. This makes steel stiffer and stronger than pure iron, yet less brittle than cast iron, which contains more carbon. To make steel, crude iron (pig iron) is smelted in a blast furnace to remove its impurities. Other elements can be added to create different varieties of steel. For example, chromium in steel stops it from rusting, while manganese makes it harder. Adding silicon to steel can make the alloy more magnetic, while nickel makes it less brittle at extremely low temperatures.

27
Co Cobalt

State: **Solid**
Discovery: 1739

● 27 ⊕ 27 ○ 32

Forms

The distinctive purplish color gives it the nickname "red cobalt."

Erythrite

Disks of pure cobalt refined in a laboratory

This shiny metal is fairly hard.

Cobaltite

These cubic crystals contain a sulfur compound of cobalt.

This silvery mineral smells like garlic when crushed due to the presence of arsenic.

Skutterudite

Medieval German miners often mistook ores of cobalt for precious metals. When they tried to purify these, the arsenic gas released made them sick. This unwanted side effect led to the name *kobold*, which is German for "goblin," a mischievous spirit.

Pure cobalt is hard and shiny, and is added to steel and other alloys to make them stronger. Alloys containing cobalt are used in the blades of **jet engines** and in **artificial joints**, such as hip and knee joints. Cobalt is one of the few elements

Uses

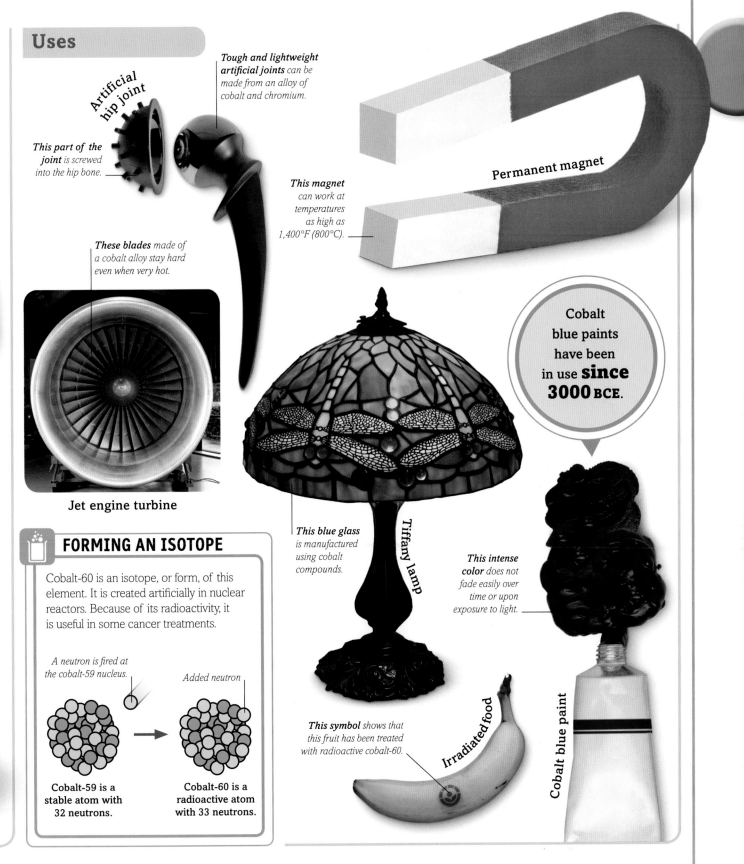

Artificial hip joint

Tough and lightweight artificial joints can be made from an alloy of cobalt and chromium.

This part of the joint is screwed into the hip bone.

These blades made of a cobalt alloy stay hard even when very hot.

Jet engine turbine

Permanent magnet

This magnet can work at temperatures as high as 1,400°F (800°C).

Cobalt blue paints have been in use **since 3000 BCE.**

This blue glass is manufactured using cobalt compounds.

Tiffany lamp

This intense color does not fade easily over time or upon exposure to light.

This symbol shows that this fruit has been treated with radioactive cobalt-60.

Irradiated food

Cobalt blue paint

FORMING AN ISOTOPE

Cobalt-60 is an isotope, or form, of this element. It is created artificially in nuclear reactors. Because of its radioactivity, it is useful in some cancer treatments.

A neutron is fired at the cobalt-59 nucleus.

Added neutron

Cobalt-59 is a stable atom with 32 neutrons.

Cobalt-60 is a radioactive atom with 33 neutrons.

that can be used to make a permanent magnet. Large **permanent magnets** are made from a tough alloy of cobalt, nickel, and aluminum, called alnico. A radioactive form of cobalt, called cobalt-60, is produced in nuclear reactors. This form is widely employed to **irradiate food**, a process by which food is exposed to a tiny dose of radiation to kill harmful germs. Cobalt can also produce a deep shade of blue: **cobalt blue paints** and dyes are formed by reacting aluminum with cobalt oxide.

65

28
Ni Nickel

Forms

State: **Solid**
Discovery: 1751
⊖ 28 ⊕ 28 ◯ 30

Garnierite

This green color comes from the presence of nickel.

Pentlandite

This reddish mineral is made of iron and nickel sulfide.

Nickeline

This nickel ore also contains arsenic.

Pure nickel balls refined in a laboratory

These silvery white metal pellets have a yellowish tinge.

Nickel is named after Old Nick, a demonic spirit from Christian lore that was believed to live underground. In the 18th century, German miners mistook a poisonous nickel mineral, now known as **nickeline**, for a copper ore. When this mineral failed to yield copper, they named it *Kupfernickel*, meaning "Old Nick's copper." Nickel is also found in other ores, such as **garnierite** and **pentlandite**. This element is one of the most useful metals, with a number of applications. Because **pure nickel** does not rust, it is used to coat objects to make

Uses

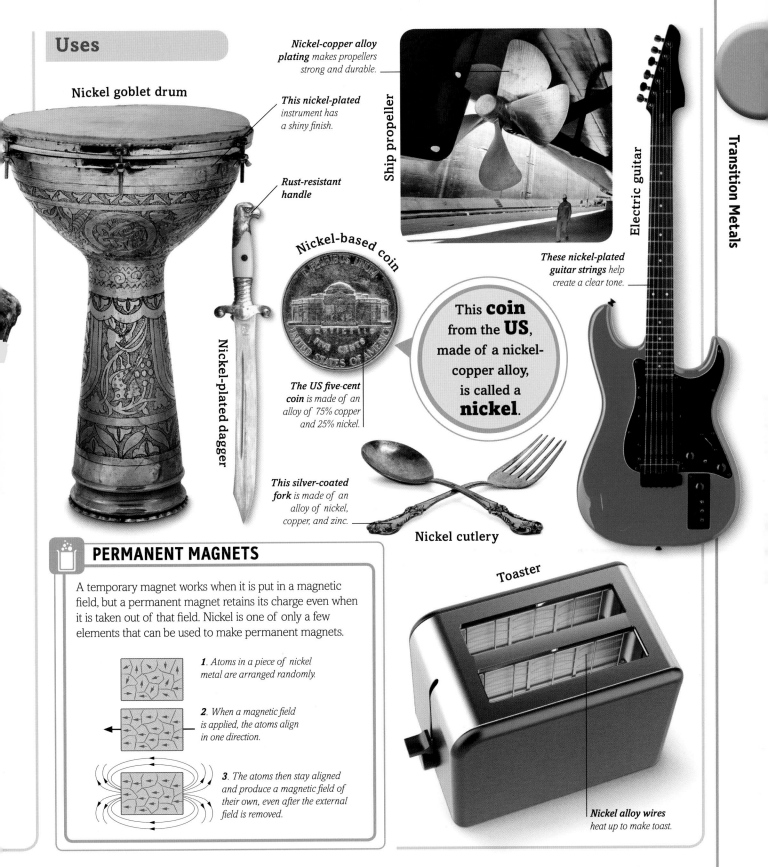

Nickel goblet drum

Nickel-copper alloy plating makes propellers strong and durable.

Ship propeller

This nickel-plated instrument has a shiny finish.

Rust-resistant handle

Nickel-based coin

Nickel-plated dagger

The US five-cent coin is made of an alloy of 75% copper and 25% nickel.

This **coin** from the **US**, made of a nickel-copper alloy, is called a **nickel**.

Electric guitar

These nickel-plated guitar strings help create a clear tone.

This silver-coated fork is made of an alloy of nickel, copper, and zinc.

Nickel cutlery

Toaster

PERMANENT MAGNETS

A temporary magnet works when it is put in a magnetic field, but a permanent magnet retains its charge even when it is taken out of that field. Nickel is one of only a few elements that can be used to make permanent magnets.

1. Atoms in a piece of nickel metal are arranged randomly.

2. When a magnetic field is applied, the atoms align in one direction.

3. The atoms then stay aligned and produce a magnetic field of their own, even after the external field is removed.

Nickel alloy wires heat up to make toast.

them look like silver—a trick still used to make inexpensive ornamental objects. Nickel is also mixed with copper to make an alloy called cupronickel. This is used as plating on **propellers** and other metallic parts of a ship because the alloy does not corrode in seawater. The same alloy is used in most of the world's silver-colored **coins**. Nickel is used in the strings of **electric guitars**. This element is added to chromium to make an alloy called nichrome. Wires made of this alloy conduct heat very well, so are used in **toasters**.

29
Cu Copper

State: **Solid**
Discovery: **Prehistoric**

− 29 + 29 ◯ 35

Forms

Copper growth on limonite

In caves, featherlike crystals are often formed.

Malachite

Unique reddish orange color

Pellets of pure copper refined in a laboratory

Branchlike crystals *of copper*

These golden yellow crystals *contain copper sulfide.*

Chalcopyrite

Colorful tarnish *develops when the mineral reacts with air.*

Bornite

Crustacean blood

Crustacean blood is blue because it contains copper.

Copper is a soft, pliable metal that is an excellent conductor of electricity and heat. Although it is one of the few elements found pure in nature, most of it exists in ores such as **chalcopyrite**. Other copper minerals, such as **malachite** and azurite, are brightly colored.

Copper is the only metal that has a reddish color in its pure form. **Pure copper** is mainly used as **wires** in electrical equipment. Copper wire wrapped around an iron core and then electrified helps create an **electromagnet**. Because they can be switched on or off, electromagnets can be

Uses

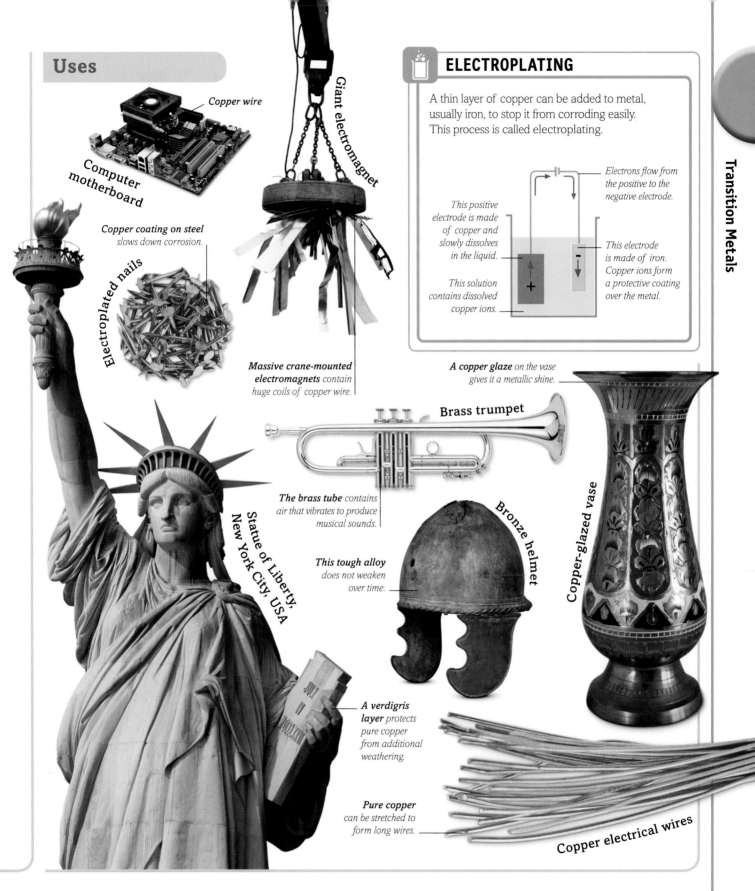

Computer motherboard

Copper wire

Giant electromagnet

Copper coating on steel *slows down corrosion.*

Electroplated nails

Massive crane-mounted electromagnets contain huge coils of copper wire.

ELECTROPLATING

A thin layer of copper can be added to metal, usually iron, to stop it from corroding easily. This process is called electroplating.

Electrons flow from the positive to the negative electrode.

This positive electrode is made of copper and slowly dissolves in the liquid.

This electrode is made of iron. Copper ions form a protective coating over the metal.

This solution contains dissolved copper ions.

A copper glaze on the vase gives it a metallic shine.

Brass trumpet

The brass tube contains air that vibrates to produce musical sounds.

Statue of Liberty, New York City, USA

This tough alloy does not weaken over time.

Bronze helmet

Copper-glazed vase

A verdigris layer protects pure copper from additional weathering.

Pure copper can be stretched to form long wires.

Copper electrical wires

magnetic as and when they are needed. They can be much more powerful than normal magnets and can lift heavy objects. Pure copper does not rust, but it reacts with air over time to form a layer of gray-green copper carbonate called verdigris. This can be seen on copper statues, such as the **Statue of Liberty**. Copper is often mixed with other metals to produce tougher alloys. Bronze, a copper-tin alloy, is more durable than pure copper and has been used since ancient times. Brass, a copper-zinc alloy, is used in musical instruments, such as **trumpets**.

69

COPPER WIRES
Not much thicker than a human hair, these copper wires are twisted together and woven into a tight bundle. One of the main uses for these wires is to shield a thicker copper wire that transmits a signal to a television. Because the signal carries pictures and sounds in the form of electrical currents, the wires wrapped around it prevent interference from other electrical sources nearby.

Copper is a very good conductor of electricity, but not the best; silver is better. However, copper is more widely used because it is much cheaper to find and purify. Each year, about 16.5 million tons (15 million metric tons) of pure copper is produced, and more than half of it is used to make electrical components, such as this mesh. Today, more than a billion miles of copper wiring is running unseen in power supplies, buildings, and electronics. Copper is now the most common electrical metal, but it has a long history. It was the first element to be refined from ores in large amounts about 7,000 years ago in the region that is now Iraq. Today, Bingham Canyon in Utah is the world's largest copper mine.

30 Zn **Zinc**

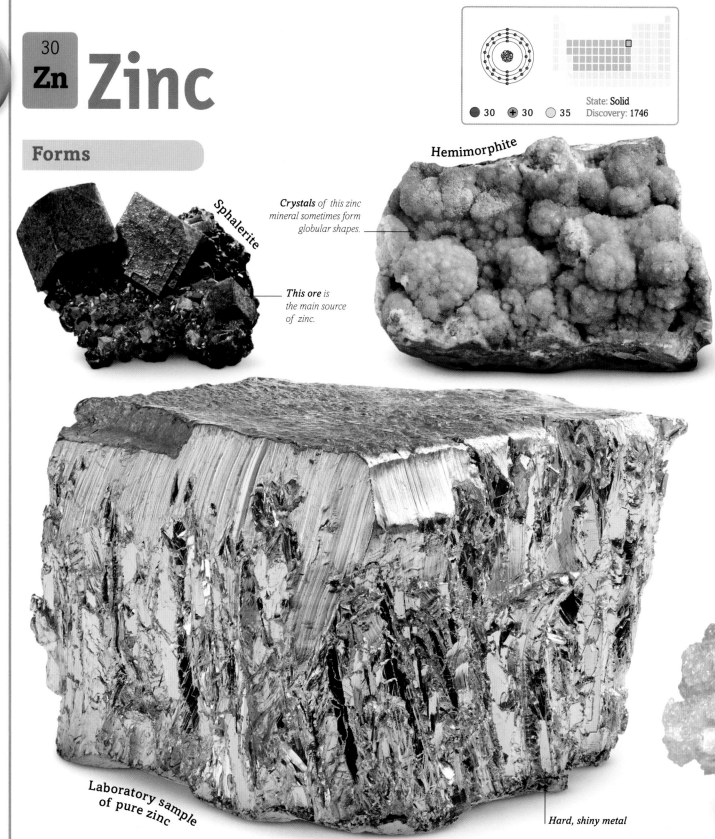

State: **Solid**
Discovery: 1746

● 30   ⊕ 30   ○ 35

Forms

Sphalerite

Crystals *of this zinc mineral sometimes form globular shapes.*

Hemimorphite

This ore *is the main source of zinc.*

Laboratory sample of pure zinc

Hard, shiny metal

Zinc was used in India and China hundreds of years before the German chemist Andreas Marggraf identified it as a new element in the 18th century. This element is a transition metal that is never pure in nature, but is found in many minerals. The mineral **sphalerite**, containing zinc sulfide, is the major source of **pure zinc**. Another principal mineral, **hemimorphite**, contains zinc and silicon. Zinc is essential in our diet. We consume it from food such as cheese and sunflower seeds. Zinc compounds have a wide

Supernova

Along with many other elements, zinc atoms are formed inside supernovae (exploding giant stars).

Smithsonite

Smithsonite was discovered by James Smithson, the founder of the **Smithsonian** Institution.

This mineral contains zinc carbonate.

Zincite

Zinc oxide crystals are generally colorless.

Uses

First-aid tape

Medical tapes that contain zinc oxide stop wounds from getting infected with microbes.

The zinc coating on this steel bridge protects it from rust.

Akashi Kaikyo Bridge, Kobe, Japan

US penny

This zinc coin is coated with copper.

Rubber boots

This flexible rubber is made stronger by adding zinc oxide.

This soothing skin lotion contains a mixture of zinc compounds.

Calamine lotion

GALVANIZED STEEL

Steel is protected from corrosion by coating it with zinc. Alloys of iron and zinc form in layers between the steel and pure zinc. This process is called galvanization.

Pure zinc

94% zinc and 6% iron

90% zinc and 10% iron

Steel is an alloy of iron and carbon.

range of applications. For example, a compound of zinc and oxygen called zinc oxide is used in **medical tape** and sunscreen. Zinc oxide can also be used to toughen the rubber used in **boots** and tires. A compound of zinc and sulfur called zinc sulfide is used to make some paints that glow in the dark. When pure zinc is exposed to air, the metal reacts with oxygen to form a protective layer of an oxide. This coating can prevent objects covered in zinc, such as **bridges**, from corroding easily.

39 Y Yttrium

State: **Solid**
Discovery: 1794
− 39   + 39   ○ 50

Forms

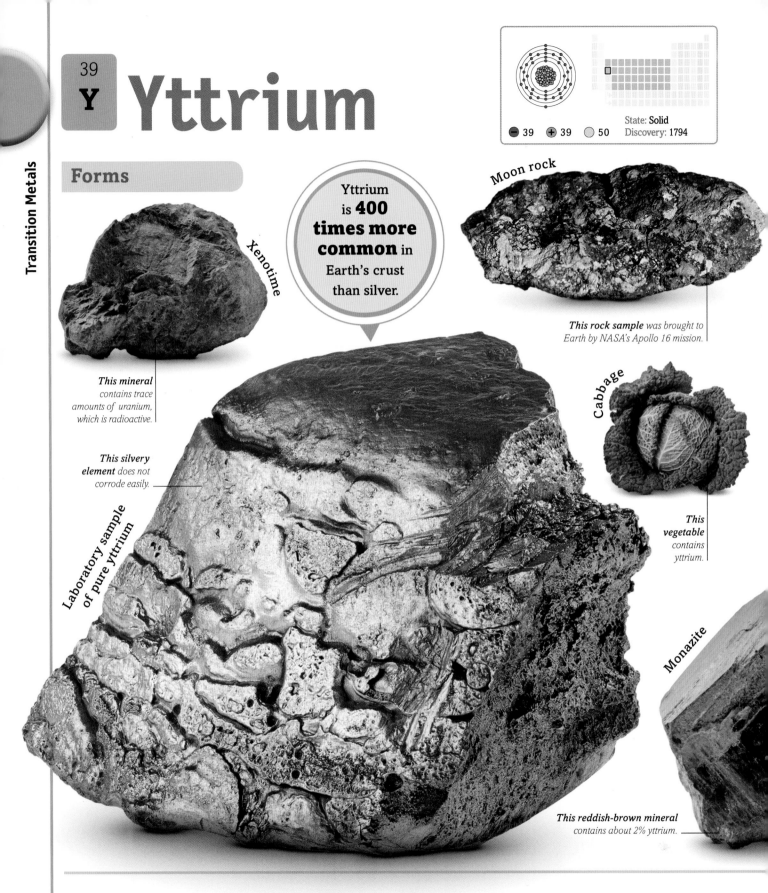

Xenotime

This mineral *contains trace amounts of uranium, which is radioactive.*

Yttrium is **400 times more common** in Earth's crust than silver.

Moon rock

This rock sample *was brought to Earth by NASA's Apollo 16 mission.*

This silvery element *does not corrode easily.*

Laboratory sample of pure yttrium

Cabbage

This vegetable *contains yttrium.*

Monazite

This reddish-brown mineral *contains about 2% yttrium.*

The samples of rock brought back from the Moon by astronauts in NASA's Apollo missions contained higher levels of yttrium than rocks on Earth. This element is never found in pure form in nature, but small traces of it are present in many minerals, including **xenotime** and **monazite**. Yttrium was discovered in a compound in 1794 by the Finnish chemist Johan Gadolin, but it wasn't isolated until 1828. Other yttrium compounds have since been found in vegetables, including **cabbage**, and in seeds of woody plants. In

Uses

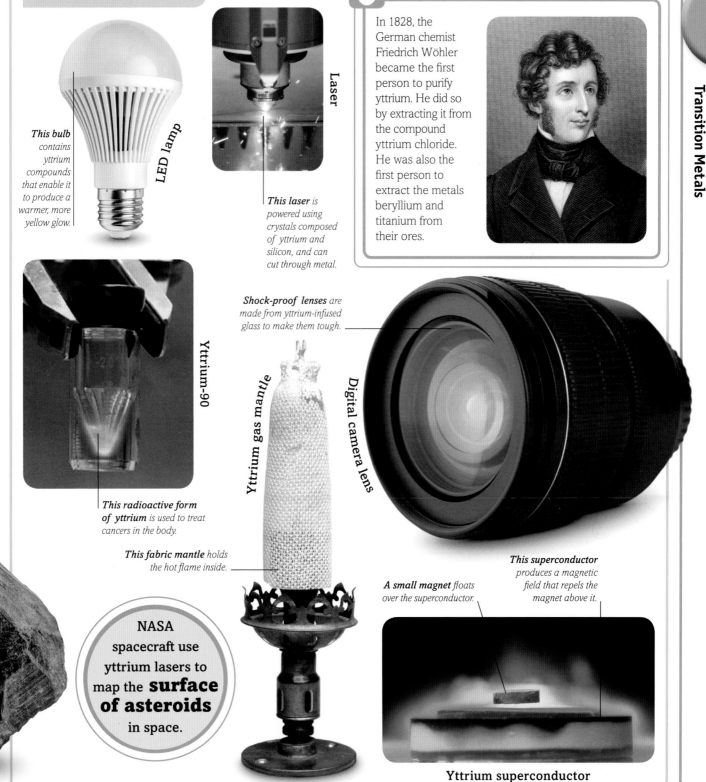

This bulb contains yttrium compounds that enable it to produce a warmer, more yellow glow.

LED lamp

Laser

This laser is powered using crystals composed of yttrium and silicon, and can cut through metal.

FRIEDRICH WÖHLER

In 1828, the German chemist Friedrich Wöhler became the first person to purify yttrium. He did so by extracting it from the compound yttrium chloride. He was also the first person to extract the metals beryllium and titanium from their ores.

Yttrium-90

This radioactive form of yttrium is used to treat cancers in the body.

Shock-proof lenses are made from yttrium-infused glass to make them tough.

Yttrium gas mantle

Digital camera lens

This fabric mantle holds the hot flame inside.

NASA spacecraft use yttrium lasers to **map the surface of asteroids** in space.

This superconductor produces a magnetic field that repels the magnet above it.

A small magnet floats over the superconductor.

Yttrium superconductor

LED lamps, yttrium converts blue light to other colors. Many **lasers** use an artificial mixture of yttrium and aluminum inside a silicon-rich crystal called garnet. Powerful yttrium lasers are used for treating some skin infections, as well as by dentists during tooth surgery. A radioactive form of this element has medical applications. Yttrium is added to the glass in a **camera lens** to make it tough. Yttrium compounds are also used in **superconductors**—materials that conduct electricity easily when cooled to very low temperatures.

40 Zr Zirconium

State: **Solid**
Discovery: 1789
● 40 ✚ 40 ○ 51

Forms

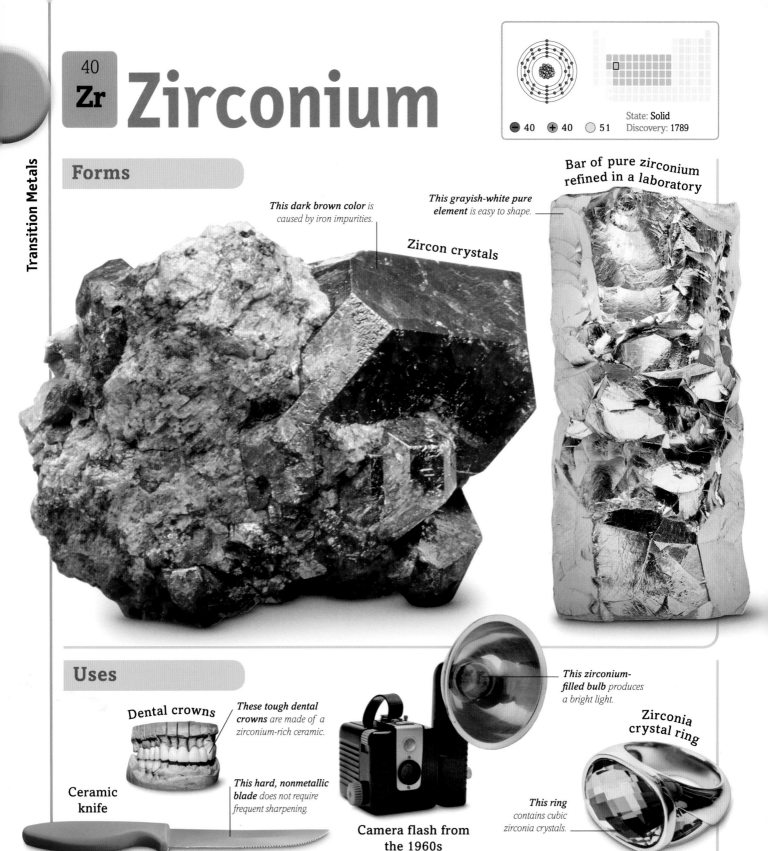

This dark brown color is caused by iron impurities.

This grayish-white pure element is easy to shape.

Zircon crystals

Bar of pure zirconium refined in a laboratory

Uses

Dental crowns

These tough dental crowns are made of a zirconium-rich ceramic.

Ceramic knife

This hard, nonmetallic blade does not require frequent sharpening.

This zirconium-filled bulb produces a bright light.

Camera flash from the 1960s

Zirconia crystal ring

This ring contains cubic zirconia crystals.

This element is named after the mineral **zircon**, which means "golden" in Persian, a reference to the golden-brown color of its crystals. The Swedish chemist Jacob Berzelius was the first person to isolate **pure zirconium**, in 1824. Today, however, the element is mostly used in the form of the compound zirconium dioxide, or zirconia. Powdered zirconia is heated to produce a hard glasslike ceramic, which is used to create **dental crowns** and sharp **ceramic knives**. Powdered zirconia also forms sparkling **zirconia crystals** that look like diamonds.

41 Nb Niobium

State: **Solid**
Discovery: 1801

⊖ 41   ⊕ 41   ◯ 52

Forms

This dark, dense ore has a light metallic shine.

Columbite

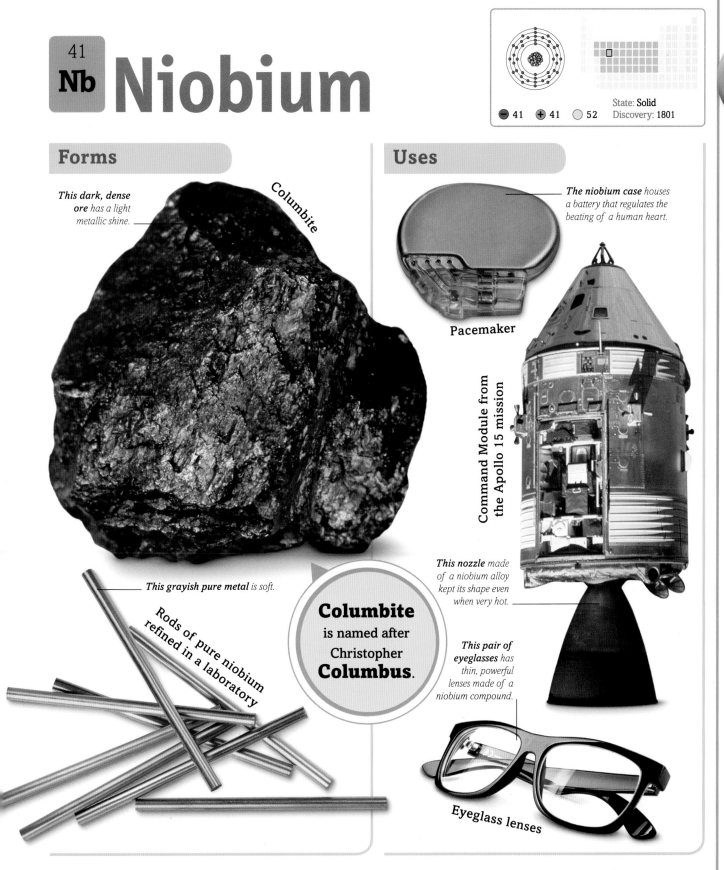

This grayish pure metal is soft.

Rods of pure niobium refined in a laboratory

Columbite is named after Christopher **Columbus**.

Uses

The niobium case houses a battery that regulates the beating of a human heart.

Pacemaker

Command Module from the Apollo 15 mission

This nozzle made of a niobium alloy kept its shape even when very hot.

This pair of eyeglasses has thin, powerful lenses made of a niobium compound.

Eyeglass lenses

Niobium is so similar to the metal tantalum that the two were wrongly thought to be the same element for almost 40 years. The mineral **columbite** is the main source of this shiny metal. Niobium is not found naturally in its **pure form**. When extracted, it has many uses. As the element does not react adversely in the human body, it is used in implants, such as **pacemakers**. Niobium also does not expand when hot, so it is used to make parts of rockets, such as the one on the **Command Module** from NASA's Apollo 15 spacecraft that went to the Moon in 1971.

42
Mo Molybdenum

Forms

This mineral feels greasy to the touch.

Molybdenite

This metal's pure form is silver-gray and has a very high melting point: 4,753°F (2,623°C).

Chunk of pure molybdenum refined in a laboratory

Uses

This slippery lubricant, which contains finely powdered molybdenite mixed with oil, protects fast-moving mechanical parts in engines.

Lubricant

This lightweight but stiff frame is made from a steel containing molybdenum and chromium.

Chrome-Moly steel bike

These closely fitting parts are hard so they do not get damaged easily.

Ratchet set

Molybdenum gets its unusual name from the Greek word *molybdos*, which means "lead." Miners once mistook **molybdenite**, a dark mineral containing this metal, for an ore of lead. This element is much harder than lead, so it is easy to distinguish between these two elements when they are pure. Molybdenite is soft and slippery, and it is the main molybdenum ore. **Pure molybdenum** is mainly used to make alloys that are resistant to corrosion. These are lightweight so are ideal for constructing **bike frames**, but

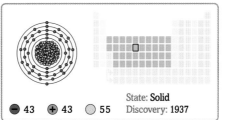

- 42 + 42 ○ 54

State: **Solid**
Discovery: 1781

43 Tc Technetium

- 43 + 43 ○ 55

State: **Solid**
Discovery: 1937

This pure form of the metal is produced inside nuclear reactors.

This body scan was created using the radioactive effects of technetium.

Foil of pure technetium produced in a reactor

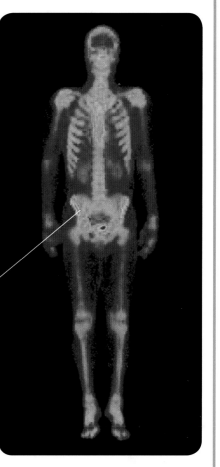

Technetium-based imaging

This experimental sports car is built with a rust-resistant alloy that contains molybdenum.

Vencer Sarthe

This box contains radioactive molybdenum, which breaks down into technetium.

Generating technetium

are hard enough for making sturdy tools, too. Molybdenum alloys are used in the latest designs of supercars such as the **Vencer Sarthe**.

Technetium was the first element to be produced artificially by researchers. It is named after the Greek word for artificial, *tekhnetos*. Technetium does not exist in nature: any of its atoms that once existed on Earth broke down millions of years ago. Tiny amounts of this element were discovered in the waste produced by early nuclear reactors. Technetium is the lightest radioactive element. It is used extensively in **medical imaging**. It is injected into a patient's body, where it emits radiation for a short time. Some machines use this radiation to show bones clearly.

44
Ru Ruthenium

State: **Solid**
Discovery: 1844

– 44   + 44   ○ 57

Forms

Pentlandite

These crystals have a bright, silver color.

This yellow-brown mineral is often found deep underground.

Pure ruthenium refined in a laboratory

Uses

Electronic circuit board

This component contains ruthenium dioxide.

Toggle switch

The metal alloy in the switch is toughened by adding ruthenium.

These low-cost solar panels are made using ruthenium.

SwissTech Convention Center, Switzerland

Ruthenium is named after *Ruthenia*, an old Latin name for Russia. This rare metal is found in the mineral **pentlandite**, and its **pure form** is commonly extracted from this ore. A compound called ruthenium dioxide is used in several components in **electronic** circuits, including resistors and microchips for computers and other digital devices. Adding a small amount of ruthenium makes softer metals, such as platinum and palladium, much tougher. Moving parts in devices such as **switches** benefit from this property.

45
Rh Rhodium

State: **Solid**
Discovery: 1803

−45 +45 ○58

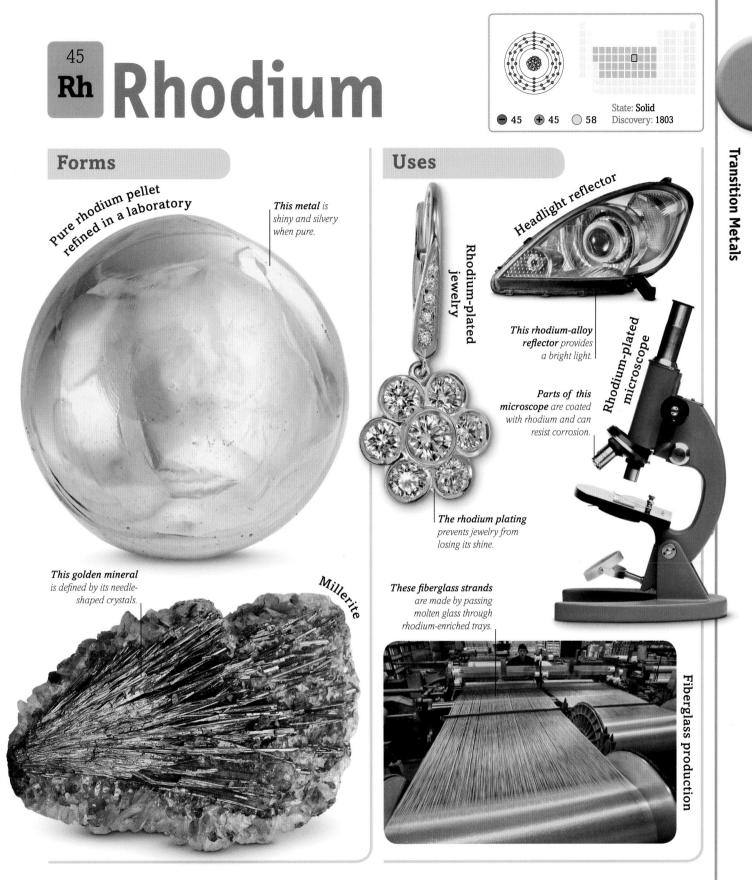

Forms

Pure rhodium pellet refined in a laboratory

This metal *is shiny and silvery when pure.*

This golden mineral *is defined by its needle-shaped crystals.*

Millerite

Uses

Headlight reflector

Rhodium-plated jewelry

This rhodium-alloy reflector *provides a bright light.*

Parts of this microscope *are coated with rhodium and can resist corrosion.*

Rhodium-plated microscope

The rhodium plating *prevents jewelry from losing its shine.*

These fiberglass strands *are made by passing molten glass through rhodium-enriched trays.*

Fiberglass production

The rosy red color of one of its compounds inspired the name rhodium. The Greek word *rhodon* means "rose-colored." Rhodium is unreactive and does not form compounds easily. It is a rare metal. Most of the **pure form** is extracted when platinum is mined. Pure rhodium is hard and is used to toughen precious **jewelry**, mirrors, and optical devices, such as **microscopes**. It is mainly used in the production of catalytic convertors for cars. **Fiberglass**, which is often found in protective gear—like helmets—also contains rhodium.

46
Pd Palladium

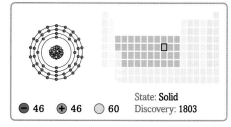

−46　＋46　○60

State: **Solid**
Discovery: 1803

Forms

The mines in this area have a high concentration of palladium.

Palladium absorbs **hydrogen** like a sponge soaking up water.

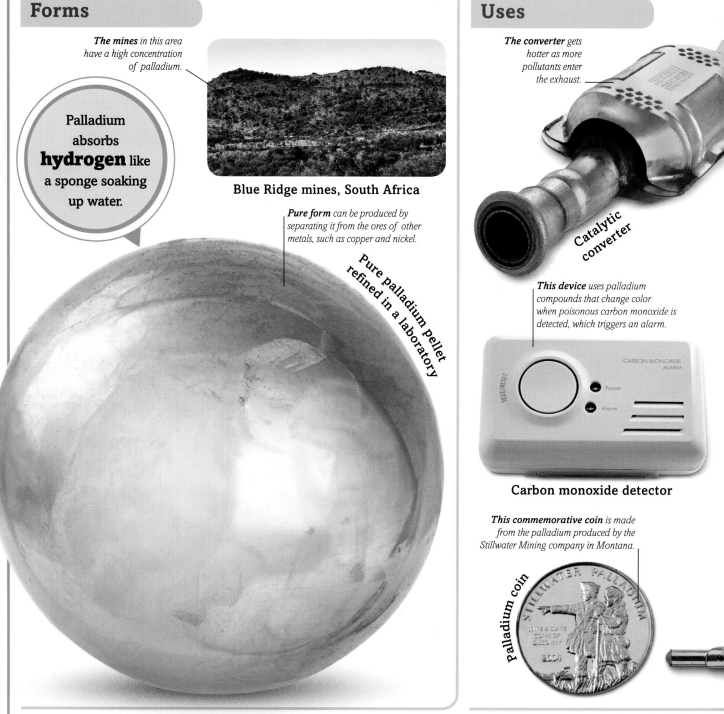

Blue Ridge mines, South Africa

Pure form can be produced by separating it from the ores of other metals, such as copper and nickel.

Pure palladium pellet refined in a laboratory

Uses

The converter gets hotter as more pollutants enter the exhaust.

Catalytic converter

This device uses palladium compounds that change color when poisonous carbon monoxide is detected, which triggers an alarm.

Carbon monoxide detector

This commemorative coin is made from the palladium produced by the Stillwater Mining company in Montana.

Palladium coin

Palladium is a rare, precious metal: it is 10 times rarer than silver and twice as rare as gold. Like these metals, palladium has a shiny surface and does not corrode easily. Palladium is found **pure** in nature, but it also has a few rare minerals, such as braggite. Of its many applications, the element's main use is in **catalytic converters**, which are devices used in vehicles to convert poisonous exhaust gases into less harmful ones. A compound called palladium chloride is used in **carbon monoxide detectors**. Because the element is

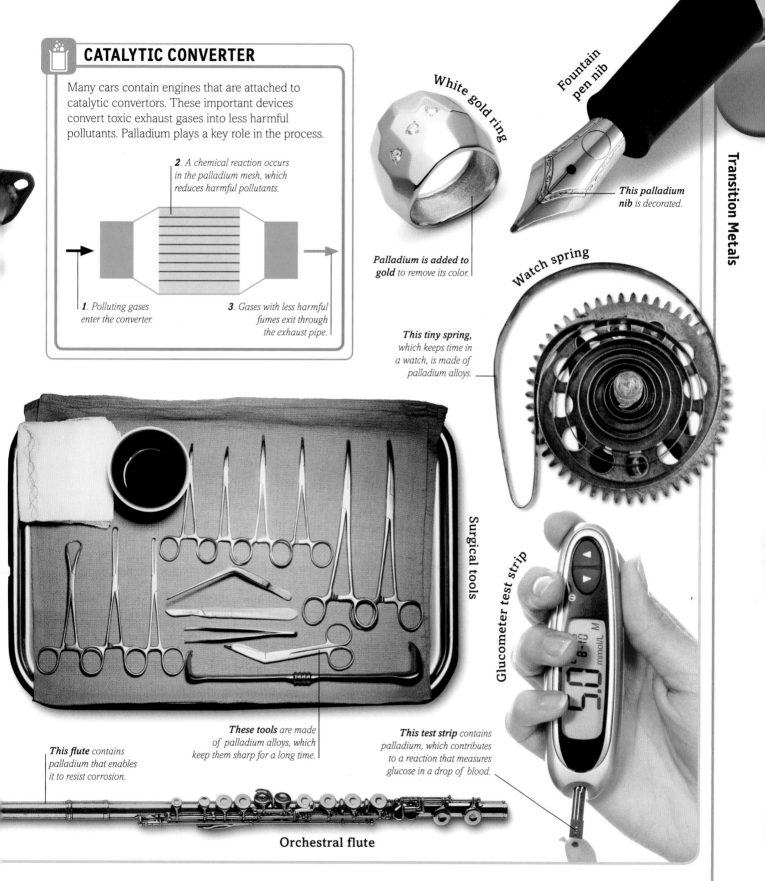

CATALYTIC CONVERTER

Many cars contain engines that are attached to catalytic convertors. These important devices convert toxic exhaust gases into less harmful pollutants. Palladium plays a key role in the process.

2. A chemical reaction occurs in the palladium mesh, which reduces harmful pollutants.

1. Polluting gases enter the converter.

3. Gases with less harmful fumes exit through the exhaust pipe.

White gold ring

Fountain pen nib

This palladium nib is decorated.

Palladium is added to gold to remove its color.

Watch spring

This tiny spring, which keeps time in a watch, is made of palladium alloys.

Surgical tools

Glucometer test strip

This test strip contains palladium, which contributes to a reaction that measures glucose in a drop of blood.

These tools are made of palladium alloys, which keep them sharp for a long time.

This flute contains palladium that enables it to resist corrosion.

Orchestral flute

precious, it is used to make **commemorative coins** in some countries. Palladium is alloyed with steel to make it more resistant to corrosion. These alloys are used to make **surgical tools** and expensive musical instruments, such as some **flutes**. Palladium is often mixed with gold to form an alloy called white gold, which is used in jewelry. Some fountain pens have **nibs** decorated with palladium. The element is also used in **glucometer test strips** so that patients can check the level of glucose in their blood.

47
Ag Silver

State: **Solid**
● 47 ⊕ 47 ○ 61 Discovery: **c. 3000** BCE

Forms

This mineral's color changes to purple when it is exposed to bright light.

Chlorargyrite

Pyrargyrite

0.03 oz (1 g) of silver can be drawn into a **1.2- mile- (2-km-) long** wire.

The bright surface tarnishes after reacting with air.

Chunk of silver

These large opaque crystals have a glistening sheen.

Acanthite

Black silver sulfide forms twisted crystals.

Silver gets its symbol "Ag" from its Latin name *argentum*, which means "shiny white." It is considered a precious metal because its pure form has a gray shine that does not corrode quickly, and it stays untarnished if cleaned regularly. Silver can be found pure in nature, but mostly it is mined from ores, such as **pyrargyrite** and **acanthite**. Because this element is valuable and can be molded easily, pure silver was used historically to make **coins**. This metal is also ideal for making **bracelets** and settings for gems. Some people even use

Uses

MAKING CLOUDS

Rain is crucial to our Earth, especially for growing healthy crops. Where there are no clouds, scientists can form tiny water droplets that cling to silver iodide powder, forming artificial rain clouds.

1. Aircraft releases silver iodide powder.

2. Ice and water droplets produce a cloud.

3. Rain falls when the water droplets in a cloud become heavy enough.

Silver coating is used on some circuit board parts.

Circuit board

Silver coin

Soft silver is easily pressed into coins.

The polished surface has a pale, metallic shine.

Antique silver spoon

Edible silver foil

These thin sheets of silver called "vark" are edible.

Pure silver molded and cut into varying shapes

Silver bracelet

Silver nitrate is mixed with water to clean cuts and abrasions.

SILVER NITRATE (V) AgNO₃

Silver nitrate

Glass infused with silver chloride turns brownish when exposed to sunlight.

Photochromatic glasses

Photography plate

An image forms when silver bromide darkens quickly on exposure to light.

flattened **silver foil** to decorate food. **Silver spoons** and forks were the only utensils that did not create a nasty metallic flavor in the mouth in the days before the invention of stainless steel. Silver conducts electricity better than copper, and is used in some

circuit boards. **Silver nitrate** (a compound of silver, nitrogen, and oxygen) is a mild disinfectant used in some antibacterial soaps. Silver forms light-sensitive compounds with chlorine (used in **sunglasses**) and bromine (used in old **photography plates**).

48 Cd Cadmium

State: Solid
Discovery: 1817

− 48   + 48   ○ 64

Forms

This mineral contains a rare form of cadmium sulfide, a compound of cadmium and sulfur.

This soft metal has a bluish tinge.

Pellet of pure cadmium refined in a laboratory

Greenockite

The yellow color of this zinc mineral is due to cadmium impurities.

Smithsonite

Uses

Nickel-cadmium battery

Cadmium and nickel layers create electricity in this rechargeable battery.

This deep red pigment contains powdered cadmium oxide.

This electronic component used in circuits contains a compound of cadmium and sulfur.

Red paint containing cadmium

Light-sensitive resistor

Cadmium-covered screws do not rust.

Cadmium-plated screws

This research sample is being viewed under ultraviolet (UV) light produced by a cadmium laser.

Fluorescent microscope

Cadmium is a highly toxic metal, and is known to cause cancer. This rare element is found in the ore **greenockite**, but it is mostly obtained as a by-product of zinc extraction. **Cadmium** was discovered in 1817 from a mineral called calamine. Today, this metal is mainly used in conjunction with nickel in **rechargeable batteries**. The compound cadmium oxide was once used in preparing **red paints**, but not anymore because of its toxicity. Cadmium is also used to create lasers for use in powerful **microscopes**.

72 Hf Hafnium

State: **Solid**
− 72 + 72 ○ 106   Discovery: 1923

Forms

Zircon crystals

Hafnium uses up 4% of the mass of this zircon crystal.

A zircon crystal can be up to **4 billion years** old.

Laboratory sample of pure hafnium

This element's pure form is resistant to corrosion in air.

Uses

Sections of this cutter are made of hafnium.

Small electronic components in this microchip contain hafnium.

Metal cutter

Microchip

Hafnium is named after *Hafnia*, the Latin word for the city of Copenhagen in Denmark. It took a long time to distinguish hafnium from zirconium because the two elements are present together in crystals of the mineral **zircon** and their atoms are similar sizes. Hafnium is used in powerful **cutters** that pierce metallic objects with a hot stream of sparks. It is also used to make ultrasmall electronics—only a few millionths of a millimeter wide— in **microchips**.

73
Ta Tantalum

State: **Solid**
Discovery: 1802
— 73   + 73   ○ 108

Forms

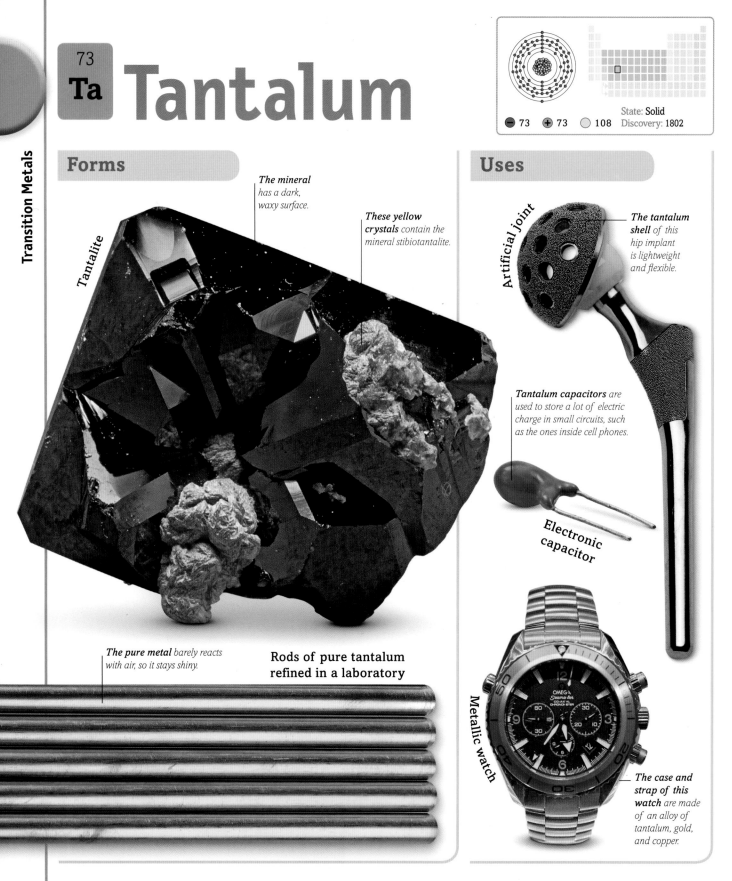

Tantalite

The mineral has a dark, waxy surface.

These yellow crystals contain the mineral stibiotantalite.

The pure metal barely reacts with air, so it stays shiny.

Rods of pure tantalum refined in a laboratory

Uses

Artificial joint

The tantalum shell of this hip implant is lightweight and flexible.

Tantalum capacitors are used to store a lot of electric charge in small circuits, such as the ones inside cell phones.

Electronic capacitor

Metallic watch

The case and strap of this watch are made of an alloy of tantalum, gold, and copper.

Tantalum is a hard metal named after Tantalus, a man from Greek mythology who was punished by the gods. It is extracted from a rare mineral called **tantalite**. This tough metal is not harmful to the human body, so it is used to make **artificial joints** and other body implants. Tantalum powder is used in **capacitors**—devices used in electronic circuits to store electricity. This strong metal toughens **watches** made of softer, precious metals. Tantalum is also used to create strong turbine blades that do not corrode.

74 W Tungsten

State: **Solid**
− 74   + 74   ○ 110   Discovery: 1783

Forms

This dark, metallic mineral contains tungsten and iron.

Ferberite

This mineral is the main source of pure tungsten.

Wolframite

Pure tungsten is a hard, gray metal.

Cylinder of pure tungsten refined in a laboratory

Uses

Drill bit

This drill bit has a coating of tungsten carbide, which protects it from damage.

Tungsten pigments were in use in Chinese porcelain 350 years ago.

Light bulb

Tungsten filaments are becoming less popular as they are not energy-efficient.

Fishing sinker

A tungsten sinker is preferred to a lead one because it is not poisonous.

Tungsten has the highest melting point of any metal: it turns to liquid at a searing 6,177.2°F (3,414°C). It is a very dense metal, and its name comes from the Swedish phrase for "heavy stone." This metal is usually obtained from the mineral **wolframite**. The compound tungsten carbide is used to harden objects such as **drill bits**. Tungsten's high melting point allows it to be used in the filaments of **light bulbs**. This element is also useful in producing weights, such as **sinkers** used with fishing lures.

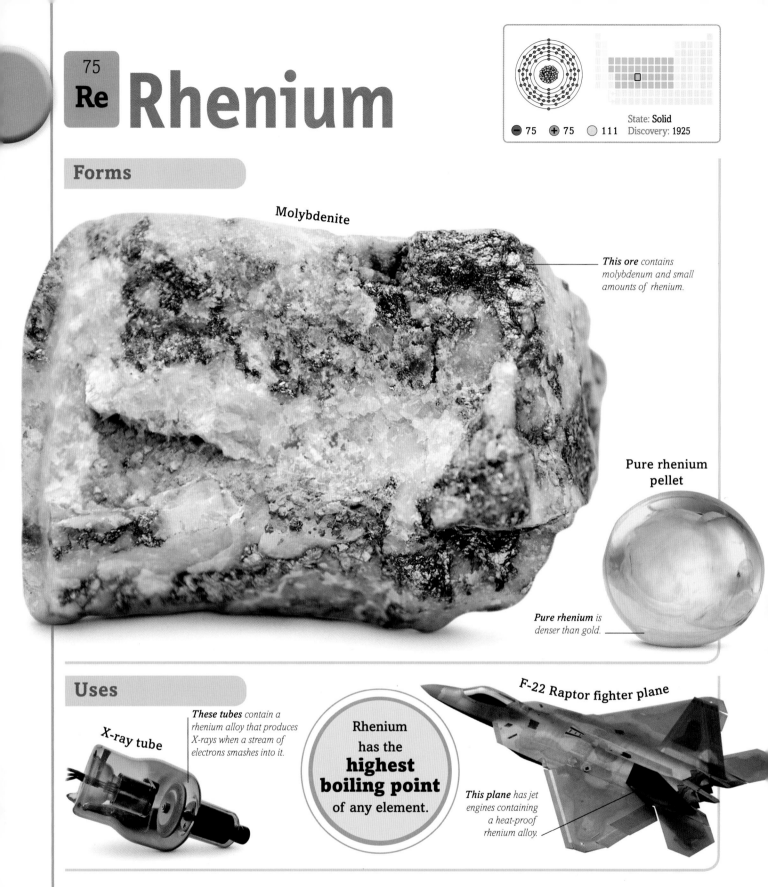

State: **Solid**
- 75 + 75 ○ 111 Discovery: **1925**

Forms

Molybdenite

This ore contains molybdenum and small amounts of rhenium.

Pure rhenium pellet

Pure rhenium is denser than gold.

Uses

These tubes contain a rhenium alloy that produces X-rays when a stream of electrons smashes into it.

X-ray tube

Rhenium has the **highest boiling point** of any element.

F-22 Raptor fighter plane

This plane has jet engines containing a heat-proof rhenium alloy.

Rhenium is very rare in nature: only one atom out of every billion in Earth's crust is a rhenium atom. Discovered in Germany in 1925, and named after the Rhine River, it was the last stable, nonradioactive element to be found. Rhenium has a very high melting point, and can stay solid at extreme temperatures. This allows alloys made of this element to be used in very hot conditions, such as those inside the tubes of **X-ray machines**, as well those in the exhaust nozzles of rockets and the jet engines of **fighter planes**.

76 Os Osmium

State: **Solid**
Discovery: 1803

⊖ 76   ⊕ 76   ◯ 114

Forms

Osmiridium sand

This is a natural alloy of osmium and iridium.

The pure form is hard but shatters easily.

Pellet of pure osmium refined in a laboratory

Uses

Transmission electron microscope (TEM) image

Osmium oxide is used to highlight objects inside a cell.

Fingerprint powder in use

Black osmium oxide powder clings to oily fingerprints.

Record player

The needle of this old record player is made of osmium.

Fountain pen

The nib of this pen moves smoothly because of its hardy osmium alloy.

Osmium is the densest of all naturally occurring elements: 8.5 fl oz (250 ml) of this metal (in its liquid form) weighs 12 lb (5.5 kg). This rare element is found in the ore **osmiridium**. **Pure osmium** reacts with oxygen in the air to form a poisonous oxide, so the metal is used safely by combining it with other elements or alloys. A red osmium oxide stains cells so they can be seen clearly under a powerful **microscope**, while a black oxide powder allows **fingerprints** to be revealed in crime investigations. A hard osmium alloy is used in **fountain pen** nibs.

77 Ir Iridium

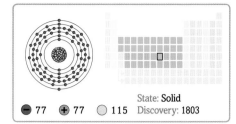

State: **Solid**
− 77 ⊕ 77 ○ 115 Discovery: 1803

Forms

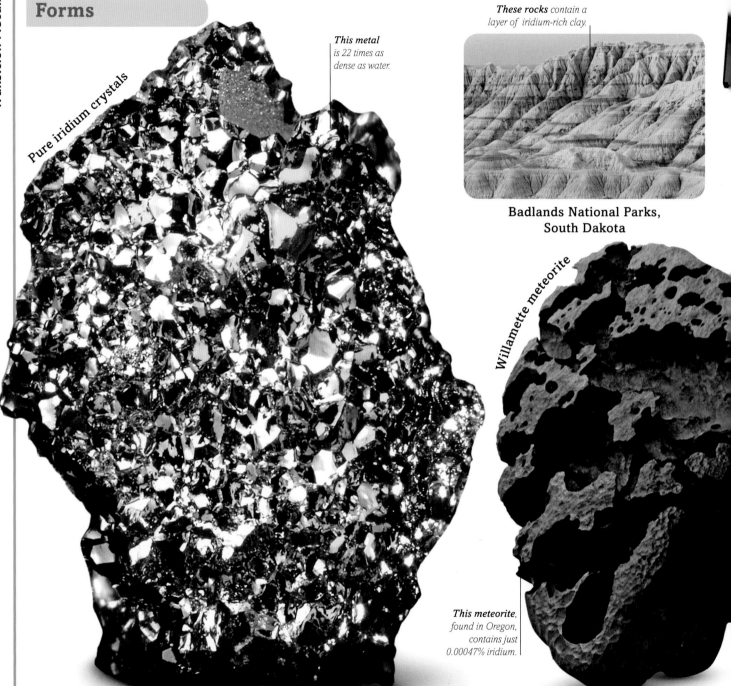

Pure iridium crystals

This metal is 22 times as dense as water.

These rocks contain a layer of iridium-rich clay.

Badlands National Parks, South Dakota

Willamette meteorite

This meteorite, found in Oregon, contains just 0.00047% iridium.

Iridium is one of the rarest natural elements on Earth: there is one iridium atom out of every billion atoms in Earth's rocks. This dense metal can be found in its **pure** form in nature as well as in other common ores that contain nickel and copper. Iridium is present in **meteorites** and other space rocks. A layer of iridium-rich clay is found in Earth's crust all over the world, especially in the **Badlands of South Dakota**. Scientists believe this small quantity of iridium in our planet's crust was deposited by the dust from an explosion 66

Uses

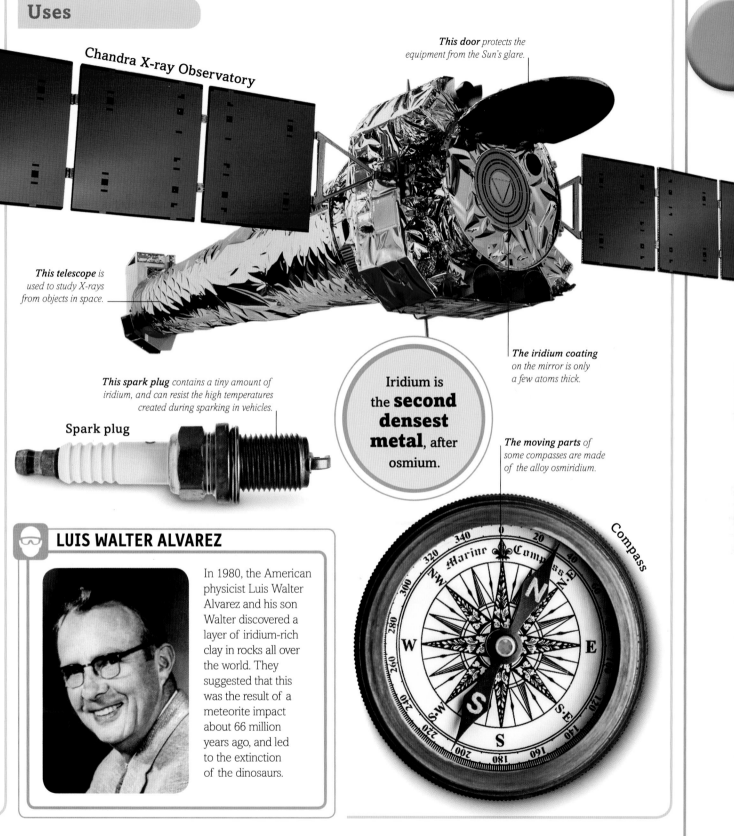

Chandra X-ray Observatory

This door protects the equipment from the Sun's glare.

This telescope is used to study X-rays from objects in space.

This spark plug contains a tiny amount of iridium, and can resist the high temperatures created during sparking in vehicles.

Spark plug

Iridium is the **second densest metal**, after osmium.

The iridium coating on the mirror is only a few atoms thick.

The moving parts of some compasses are made of the alloy osmiridium.

Compass

LUIS WALTER ALVAREZ

In 1980, the American physicist Luis Walter Alvarez and his son Walter discovered a layer of iridium-rich clay in rocks all over the world. They suggested that this was the result of a meteorite impact about 66 million years ago, and led to the extinction of the dinosaurs.

million years ago when a large meteorite hit our planet. The applications of this element include coating the mirror of NASA's **Chandra X-ray Observatory**, an Earth-orbiting telescope that studies X-rays from distant stars. Iridium is more durable than platinum and copper, and is therefore preferred over these metals for use in spark plugs. Iridium is also mixed with osmium to make an alloy called osmiridium, which is used in **compasses** and put in nibs for some fountain pens to make them hardy.

78
Pt Platinum

State: **Solid**
Discovery: **Unknown**
● 78 ⊕ 78 ○ 117

Forms

This dense, shiny mineral consisting of platinum and arsenic is the most common ore of platinum.

Platinum melts at the high temperature of **3,214°F** (1,768°C).

Sperrylite

Large nuggets of pure platinum are rare.

Nugget of pure platinum refined in a laboratory

Spanish explorers first found platinum in the mines of South America in the 1700s. They obtained a whitish substance that the locals living near there called *platina*, meaning "little silver." This precious metal has a silvery-white shine. Platinum rarely reacts with other elements, even at high temperatures. This makes it difficult to extract from its ores, such as **sperrylite**. **Pure platinum** does not corrode or tarnish. It is, however, not easy to shape or mold, so use of platinum was limited to the making of simple jewelry and **watches**. By the 20th century, more

Uses

Platinum resistance thermometer

This thermometer records temperature by measuring the electric current flowing through a fine platinum wire.

Platinum watch

Expensive watches use the precious metal platinum.

Platinum prints have a wider range of shades than silver prints.

Black and white photographic print

Jewelry made of platinum does not lose its shine.

Platinum ring

Platinum was found in an Egyptian casket from the **7th century** BCE.

This fuel cell contains platinum, which speeds up the reaction between hydrogen and oxygen.

Fuel cell

ANTONIO DE ULLOA

Although platinum had been in use in jewelry on the west coast of South America for more than 2,000 years, it was Spanish naval officer Antonio de Ulloa who made the first major study of it. In 1735, while on a South American expedition, he found grains of the metal in river sands. He brought them back to Spain to examine them.

Dental fillings once contained platinum and mercury.

This drug contains platinum and kills cancer cells in the body.

Dental crown

Cisplatin

Cancer drug

This stent made of platinum is not harmful to the body and anchors a damaged blood vessel as it heals.

Medical stent

applications were discovered. Platinum can be used in place of silver to generate **photographic prints**, and in place of gold for making **dental fillings**. Today, platinum plays an important role in various technologies. For example, it is used in **fuel cells**—devices that generate electricity by combining hydrogen and oxygen. These cells do not need to be recharged like other batteries. Powerful **drugs for treating cancer** contain this element, while **stents** made of pure platinum help heal damaged blood vessels.

79
Au Gold

State: **Solid**
⊖ 79 ⊕ 79 ○ 118 Discovery: c. 3000 BCE

Forms

Gold's chemical symbol, **Au**, comes from its **latin name**, *aurum*.

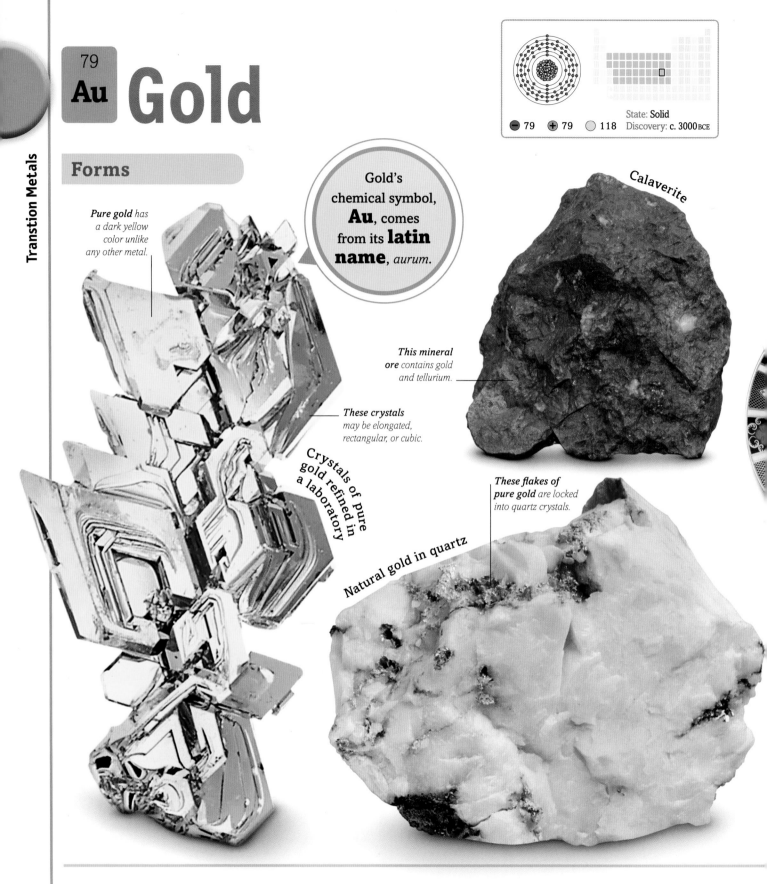

Pure gold has a dark yellow color unlike any other metal.

These crystals may be elongated, rectangular, or cubic.

Crystals of pure gold refined in a laboratory

Calaverite

This mineral ore contains gold and tellurium.

These flakes of pure gold are locked into quartz crystals.

Natural gold in quartz

People were making gold ornaments more than 6,000 years ago. This was many centuries before they learned how to purify copper, iron, and other metals. Gold is believed by many to be the first metal element to be identified. It is a dense, unreactive metal with a distinctive deep yellow color. Gold is naturally **pure** and seldom makes compounds in nature; the compound in the mineral ore **calaverite** is an exception. **Pure gold** found in nature may form nuggets but mostly is found as tiny specks embedded in rocks. Gold miners crush up these rocks and wash out the

Uses

This very thin layer of gold protects the astronaut from the Sun's heat.

Astronaut's visor

This mask was placed over the pharaoh's mummified face.

Tutankhamun's death mask

Royal Crown Derby plate

This glass plate contains specks of gold.

THE HOLTERMANN NUGGET

The largest piece of natural gold was found on October 19, 1872, near the small town of Hill End in Australia. Named after its discoverer, Bernhardt Holtermann, the piece contained more than 198 lb (90 kg) of pure gold.

4 ft 9 in (1.45 m)

Holtermann Nugget   Child aged 10 years old

Gold bars stored in banks are a sign of wealth.

FINE GOLD 999.9   NET WT 1000 g

Gold bars

Edible gold flakes

The flakes decorating this expensive chocolate are edible.

Gold teeth

These replacement teeth are made of gold and mercury.

Wat Phrathat Doi Suthep temple, Thailand

Gold foil keeps this car engine at a stable temperature.

McLaren F1 car engine

Ancient gold jewelry

A thin layer of gold covers this entire temple.

This neck ornament is made from cast gold.

gold dust with water or strong acids. The applications for gold include heat shields in **astronaut's visors**. This metal has always been seen as valuable and many ancient artifacts, such as the **3,300-year-old death mask** of Egyptian pharaoh Tutankhamun, were forged from it. Some of the earliest coins, found in Turkey, were made of it. Gold is used to cover important buildings, such as Thailand's **Wat Phrathat Doi Suthep** temple. This precious metal is most commonly used today in **jewelry** or decorations.

GOLDEN BUDDHA
A precious statue of Buddha with one thousand eyes and one thousand hands stands in Long Son Pagoda, a temple in Nha Trang, Vietnam. The Buddha is depicted holding a range of sacred objects, including scrolls and white lotus flowers. This statue is completely covered in a layer of pure gold, and it draws hundreds of devotees from across the world.

Although humans have discovered many strong metals and useful elements, gold has remained one of the most valuable. Before people knew what it was, they saw glittering gold dust in river beds or dug large gold nuggets out from rocks. They found that gold has many valuable qualities: it is soft enough to hammer into any shape and can be melted down for molding into ornaments. Best of all, its gleaming golden color never fades away. Ancient cultures prized items made of gold: in ancient Egypt, gold was used to make coins as well as to cap the tops of pyramids. Gold is, however, so rare that if all the world's mined gold were forged into a cube, it would fit inside the penalty area of a soccer field.

80
Hg Mercury

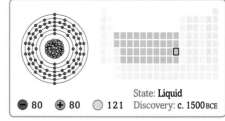

State: **Liquid**
Discovery: c. 1500 BCE

● 80   ⊕ 80   ○ 121

Forms

This bright red mineral is the main ore of mercury used today.

Cinnabar

Liquid form of pure mercury

The "ribbed" effect is due to mercury's extremely high density.

This metal melts at −38°F (−39°C).

Solid mercury is soft enough to be **cut with a knife**.

Mercury is the only metal that is liquid at room temperature. Along with water, it is one of the few liquids found naturally on Earth's surface. **Pure mercury** forms around volcanoes where the heat separates it from its minerals, such as **cinnabar**. This red mineral has been used for many centuries: Ancient Romans roasted cinnabar to release a liquid they called *hydrargyrum*, meaning "silver water." This was the element mercury. It was later known as quicksilver because of how fast it flowed as a stream of liquid. This metal is very poisonous:

100

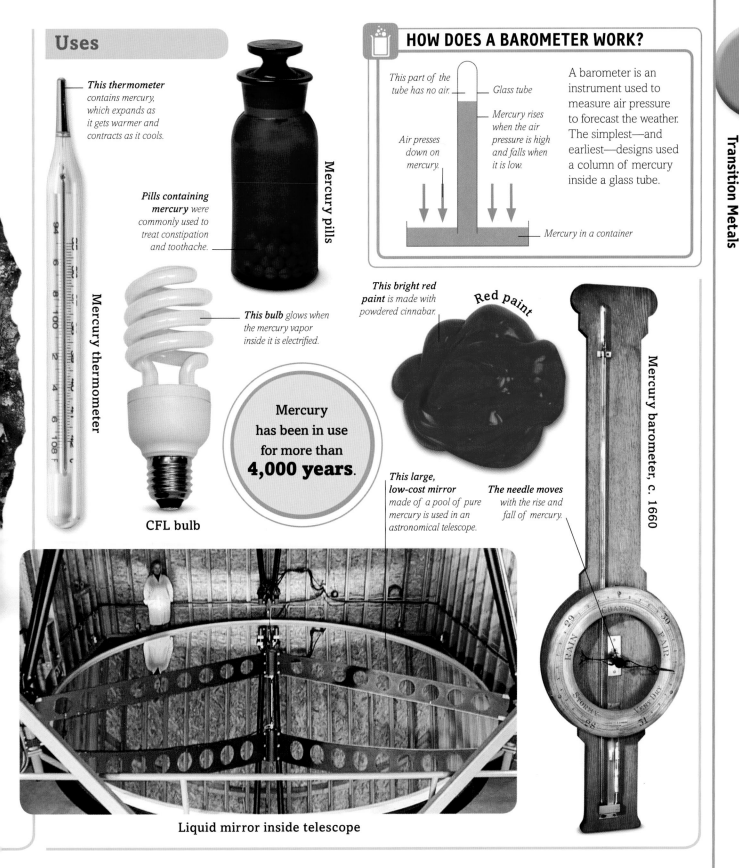

Uses

This thermometer contains mercury, which expands as it gets warmer and contracts as it cools.

Mercury thermometer

Pills containing mercury were commonly used to treat constipation and toothache.

Mercury pills

This bulb glows when the mercury vapor inside it is electrified.

CFL bulb

Mercury has been in use for more than **4,000 years**.

HOW DOES A BAROMETER WORK?

This part of the tube has no air.

Glass tube

Mercury rises when the air pressure is high and falls when it is low.

Air presses down on mercury.

Mercury in a container

A barometer is an instrument used to measure air pressure to forecast the weather. The simplest—and earliest—designs used a column of mercury inside a glass tube.

This bright red paint is made with powdered cinnabar.

Red paint

This large, low-cost mirror made of a pool of pure mercury is used in an astronomical telescope.

The needle moves with the rise and fall of mercury.

Mercury barometer, c. 1660

Liquid mirror inside telescope

it can damage organs and nerves if inhaled or swallowed. As a result, the use of this metal is carefully monitored today. Mercury is used in some batteries, some **thermometers**, and in low-energy, **compact fluorescent light (CFL) bulbs**. Its compounds are used to prepare strong, **red paints**. Until the early 18th century, mercury was used in **pills** for treating some common ailments. It gradually fell out of use when it was found to be toxic. The first accurate **barometers** also contained this liquid, but such devices are rarely seen today.

104 Rf Rutherfordium

Ernest Rutherford

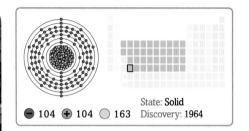

State: **Solid**
— 104 ⊕ 104 ◯ 163   Discovery: **1964**

Rutherfordium was the first superheavy element to be discovered. In this type of element, each atom has 104 or more protons in its nucleus. It is named after the New Zealand scientist **Ernest Rutherford**, who, in 1913, suggested that every atom has a nucleus, or core. Pure rutherfordium is synthesized by researchers in a laboratory.

105 Db Dubnium

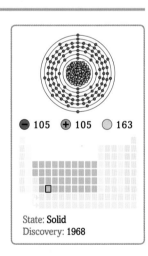

— 105 ⊕ 105 ◯ 163

State: **Solid**
Discovery: **1968**

The US scientist Albert Ghiorso discovered **12 elements** in the 20th century.

Albert Ghiorso

It took scientists nearly 30 years to agree on a name for this element. Dubnium was finally named after the Russian city of Dubna, where the first atoms of this artificial, radioactive element were created, in 1968. However, a team of American scientists led by **Albert Ghiorso** also produced samples of the element at the same time. This radioactive element has 12 isotopes, or forms, with different numbers of neutrons.

106
Sg Seaborgium

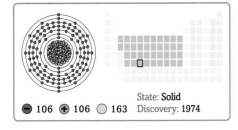

State: **Solid**
⊖ 106 ⊕ 106 ◯ 163   Discovery: 1974

Atoms of seaborgium break apart in about three minutes, so little is known about it. Scientists think it may be a metal. The element was isolated in 1974 in a machine called the **Super Heavy Ion Linear Accelerator** at the Lawrence Berkeley National Laboratory. It was named after the US chemist Glenn T. Seaborg.

This huge machine was used to discover **five new elements**.

This giant tube forms part of the Super Heavy Ion Linear Accelerator, which is a type of particle accelerator—a machine in which atoms are smashed together.

Glenn T. Seaborg

Super Heavy Ion Linear Accelerator, Lawrence Berkeley National Laboratory, California

NOBEL PRIZE IN CHEMISTRY

Glenn T. Seaborg and his fellow US researcher Edwin McMillan were awarded the Nobel Prize for Chemistry in 1951 for their work in creating neptunium. This was the first element to be isolated that was heavier than uranium—the heaviest natural element.

Nobel Prize medal

107
Bh Bohrium

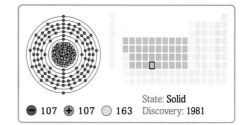

State: **Solid**
⊖ 107 ⊕ 107 ◯ 163   Discovery: **1981**

Bohrium is an artificial element named after the Danish scientist Niels Bohr. It was named for Bohr to honor his model of the structure of atoms' electron shells. Bohrium was first produced by firing chromium atoms at bismuth atoms in a particle accelerator (a machine in which atoms are smashed together). Atoms of this metal are unstable: half of any sample of bohrium atoms breaks apart in 61 seconds. As a result, it is not very well understood.

Niels Bohr

108
Hs Hassium

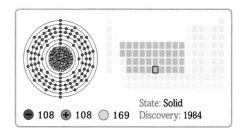

State: **Solid**
⊖ 108 ⊕ 108 ◯ 169   Discovery: **1984**

Peter Armbruster

Hassium was produced inside this chamber.

A chamber at Center for Heavy Ion Research, Darmstadt, Germany

Scientists think hassium is a metal, but they have not been able to produce enough of its atoms to study it in any detail. Hassium is very radioactive, and most of its atoms break apart within a few seconds. This element is named after the German state of Hesse, the location of the **Center for Heavy Ion Research**, where hassium was first created artificially by a team led by the German physicist **Peter Armbruster**.

109 Mt Meitnerium

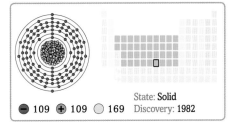

State: **Solid**
⊖ 109 ⊕ 109 ◯ 169 Discovery: 1982

Researchers think meitnerium might be the densest of all elements. It is very unstable, and even the atoms of its most stable isotope, or form, break apart in a matter of seconds. Meitnerium is named after the Austrian physicist **Lise Meitner**, to honor her achievements in physics. Several universities, such as **Humboldt University** in Berlin, Germany, also have buildings in her name.

Meitner Haus building,
Humboldt University, Germany

Lise Meitner (left) works with the German chemist Otto Hahn

110 Ds Darmstadtium

Sigurd Hofmann

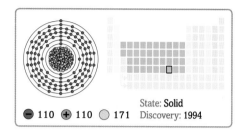

State: **Solid**
⊖ 110 ⊕ 110 ◯ 171   Discovery: 1994

This artificial element is named after the German city of Darmstadt—the home of the Institute for Heavy Ion Research where this element was first produced. A team led by the German physicist **Sigurd Hofmann** created darmstadtium by smashing nickel atoms into lead atoms in a particle accelerator (a machine in which atoms are smashed together).

111 Rg Roentgenium

Wilhem Röntgen

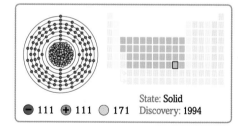

State: **Solid**
⊖ 111 ⊕ 111 ◯ 171   Discovery: 1994

Scientists believe that this metal shares many characteristics with precious metals, such as gold and silver. However, its atoms break apart within seconds, so this has not yet been confirmed. Roentgenium was created in Darmstadt, Germany. It was named after **Wilhelm Röntgen**, the German scientist who discovered X-rays in 1895.

112 Cn Copernicium

State: **Solid**
Discovery: 1996

Some scientists think copernicium could be the **only gaseous metal**.

This statue stands in front of the Polish castle in which Copernicus lived.

Statue of Nicolaus Copernicus

This German research institute is where copernicium was discovered.

Heavy Ion Research Center, Germany

The atoms of this radioactive element survive only for a few minutes, before breaking down. Copernicium is created in particle accelerators by smashing together atoms of lead and zinc. Only a few atoms of this artificial element have ever been produced. Copernicium is named after **Nicolaus Copernicus**, the Polish astronomer who theorized that our planet orbits the Sun.

107

Europium's
(Eu) colour
changes
when left
in the air.

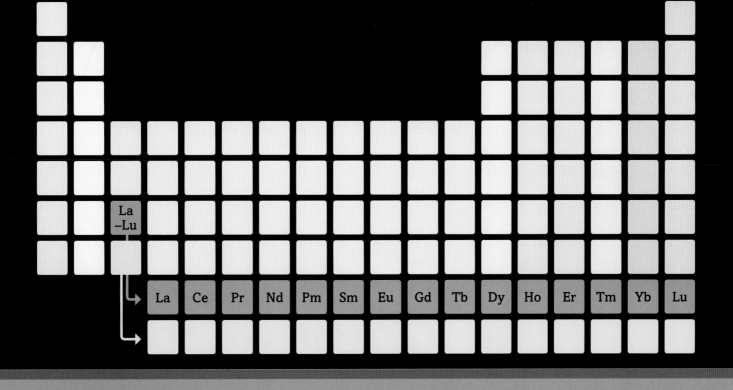

Lanthanides

This set is named after lanthanum, the first element in this series. The name "rare earth metals" is also given to these elements because they were discovered mixed together in complex minerals in Earth's crust, and were thought to be uncommon. However, they are actually not rare but abundant. These metals—between barium (Ba) and hafnium (Hf)—should fit between the alkaline earth metals and the transition metals, but are normally shown underneath the main table to save space.

Atomic structure
Atoms of every element in this group have two outer electrons. The lanthanides have large atoms, all with six electron shells.

Physical properties
The lanthanides are dense, shiny metals that tarnish easily when exposed to air. They do not conduct electricity very well.

Chemical properties
These elements react slowly with oxygen (O) at room temperature, but the reactions speed up when heated.

Compounds
Many lanthanides form compounds with oxygen called oxides. These are often used in lasers and magnets.

57
La Lanthanum

State: **Solid**
Discovery: 1839

— 57 + 57 ○ 82

Forms

Lanthanum carbonate is used to treat patients with **kidney disease**.

Bastnasite

This reddish-brown mineral *is also found in other colors, including white, tan, and gray.*

Laboratory sample of pure lanthanum

Black tarnish *forms on pure metal when it comes into contact with air.*

This metal *burns easily when ignited.*

Uses

Fluorescent lamp

This lamp *uses lanthanum to reduce the yellow color in its light.*

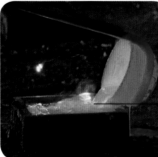

In its molten state, *lanthanum is used to smooth rough diamonds.*

Molten lanthanum

This lens *can better focus light on an object due to the presence of lanthanum oxide in the glass.*

Camera lens

Although the word "lanthanum" means "to lie hidden," it is more abundant than most metals. For example, it is three times more common than lead. This element was discovered in the mineral cerite in 1839. However, it took chemists almost another century to find a way to purify the metal. Today, the mineral **bastnasite** is a source of **pure lanthanum**. The element's applications range from its use in film studio lights and **lens-making** to refining petroleum.

58 Ce Cerium

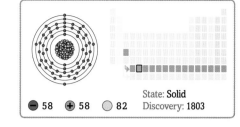

State: **Solid**
Discovery: **1803**
● 58 ⊕ 58 ○ 82

Cerium was the first of the lanthanides to be discovered. It is named after the dwarf planet Ceres, which was discovered two years before the element was isolated. Cerium is highly toxic when **pure**, but safer cerium compounds have some uses. The main use of cerium is in making phosphors, which are chemicals that produce lights of different colors. Phosphors are present in **flatscreen TVs** and bulbs.

Television

The inside of this screen is coated with cerium-containing phosphors, which emit red, green, and blue light.

Laboratory sample of pure cerium

The pure form of the metal tarnishes on contact with air.

Kitchen spatula

This red color comes from a compound called cerium sulfide.

59 Pr Praseodymium

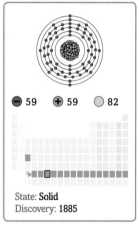

● 59 ⊕ 59 ○ 82

State: **Solid**
Discovery: **1885**

This piece of the element's pure form is often stored in mineral oil to stop it from reacting with oxygen in the air.

Part of this element's name comes from *prasinos*, the Greek word for "green." Normally a gray color when pure, the element reacts slowly on contact with air to form a green coating. Praseodymium compounds give a yellow color to glass and heat-resistant **ceramics**, and provide a green color to some **artificial jewels**. This element also boosts the strength of magnets that contain it.

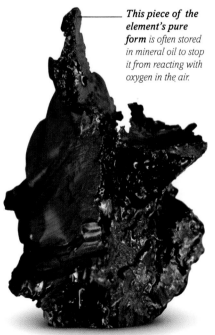

Laboratory sample of pure praseodymium

Yellow ceramic pot

This yellow color is produced by a solution containing praseodymium.

Green cubic zirconia

This artificial gem gets its green color from tiny amounts of a compound of praseodymium and oxygen.

60 Nd Neodymium

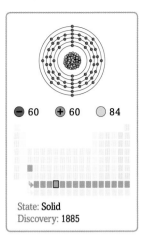

State: **Solid**
Discovery: **1885**

Pink glass

Strong magnets made of neodymium can be used to lift thousands of times their own mass. This element was discovered in 1885 by the Austrian chemist Carl Auer von Welsbach, and it was first put to use in coloring glass. Small amounts of neodymium turn **glass** pinkish purple. Today, this element is also employed in lasers used in eye surgery.

Laboratory sample of pure neodymium

This glass gets its color from very tiny amounts of neodymium.

The pure element turns black when it reacts with air.

61 Pm Promethium

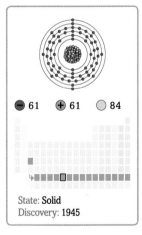

State: **Solid**
Discovery: **1945**

This paint glows as a result of radioactive promethium.

This missile uses radioactive promethium for electrical power.

Missile

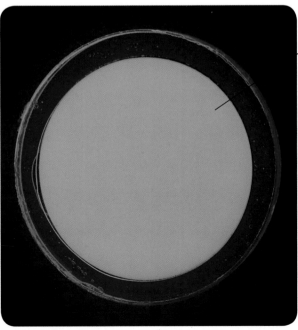

Promethium-rich paint in a can seen from above

Promethium is the rarest lanthanide element. Any promethium that was in Earth's rocks decayed billions of years ago. Promethium is therefore produced artificially in nuclear reactors. Being very radioactive, it is used in some **missiles** because it converts this radioactivity into electrical power. The addition of promethium also makes some **paints** glow in the dark.

62 Sm Samarium

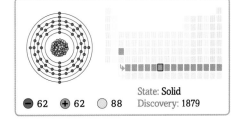

State: Solid
- 62 + 62 ○ 88
Discovery: 1879

This element is named after the mineral samarskite from which it was first purified. However, another lanthanide-rich mineral called monazite is the main source of this element today. Samarium is mixed with cobalt to make permanent magnets that are often used in **electric guitars**.

Guitar pickups

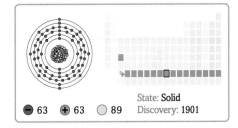

These pickups (components that sense vibrations produced by guitar strings) are made of samarium-cobalt magnets.

This silvery-white metal darkens on contact with air.

Laboratory sample of pure samarium

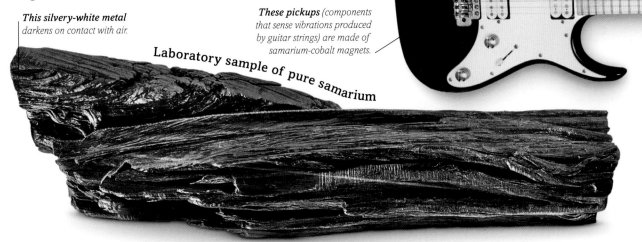

63 Eu Europium

Laboratory sample of pure europium

State: Solid
- 63 + 63 ○ 89
Discovery: 1901

Europium was named after the continent of Europe. However, most of the world's supply of the element comes from the US and China, where the mineral bastnasite is mined to extract **pure europium**. A compound called europium oxide is used in euro and **British bank notes**. When placed under ultraviolet (UV) light, the compound gives off a red glow.

This red glow proves this note is real.

The crystals of this yellowish metal often have patches of dark oxides.

Section of British note under UV light

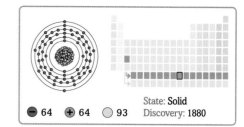

64
Gd Gadolinium

State: **Solid**
Discovery: 1880
− 64 + 64 ○ 93

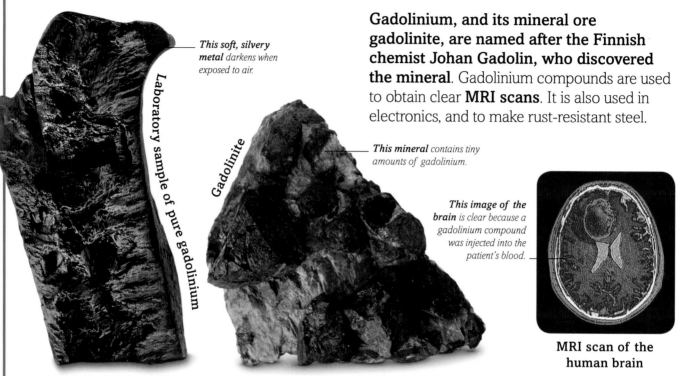

This soft, silvery metal *darkens when exposed to air.*

Laboratory sample of pure gadolinium

Gadolinite

This mineral contains tiny amounts of gadolinium.

Gadolinium, and its mineral ore gadolinite, are named after the Finnish chemist Johan Gadolin, who discovered the mineral. Gadolinium compounds are used to obtain clear **MRI scans**. It is also used in electronics, and to make rust-resistant steel.

This image of the brain is clear because a gadolinium compound was injected into the patient's blood.

MRI scan of the human brain

65
Tb Terbium

State: **Solid**
Discovery: 1843
− 65 + 65 ○ 94

Terbium is named after the village of Ytterby in Sweden. It is a silvery metal that can be obtained from the ore monazite. This element has only a few uses. **Pure terbium** is added to other metals to make powerful magnets used in sound-producing devices, such as the **SoundBug™**. Its compounds are used to line **mercury lamps**.

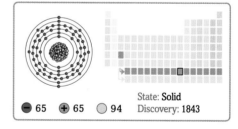

SoundBug™ device

This device uses magnets to turn any flat surface, like a window, into a loudspeaker.

The mercury vapor in this lamp produces ultraviolet light when electrified, and this is turned into a bright yellow glow by terbium.

Mercury lamp

The pure metal is soft enough to be cut with a knife.

Laboratory sample of pure terbium

66 Dy **Dysprosium**

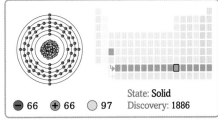

State: **Solid**
● 66 ⊕ 66 ○ 97   Discovery: **1886**

Fergusonite

This mineral contains tiny amounts of dysprosium.

This pure metal remains shiny at room temperature.

Dysprosium reacts more easily with air and water than most other lanthanide metals. Although it was discovered in 1886, it took until the 1950s to purify it. This metal is often used with neodymium to produce magnets that are used in **car motors**, wind turbines, and generators.

Some hybrid car motors contain dysprosium.

Laboratory sample of pure dysprosium

Hybrid car motor

67 Ho **Holmium**

State: **Solid**
● 67 ⊕ 67 ○ 98   Discovery: **1878**

The Swedish chemist Per Teodor Cleve named holmium after the Swedish city of Stockholm. Pure holmium can produce a strong magnetic field and is therefore used in magnets. Its compounds are used to make lasers, and to color glass and artificial jewels, such as **cubic zirconia**.

This artificial gemstone is colored red by small amounts of holmium.

Bright silver shine

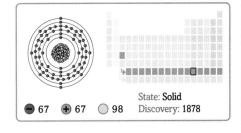

Laboratory sample of pure holmium

Red zirconia gemstone

68 Er Erbium

State: **Solid**
−68 +68 ◯99 Discovery: 1843

This silvery element slowly tarnishes on contact with air.

Laboratory sample of pure erbium

This glass contains erbium, which protects a welder's eyes from heat and bright light.

The rose-pink finish of this vase is from an erbium chloride glaze.

Pink pottery

Welding goggles

Like terbium and ytterbium, erbium is also named after the Swedish village of Ytterby, near where it was discovered. This element does not occur in its **pure form** in nature, but it can be obtained from the mineral monazite. Many erbium compounds are pink in color and are used to color **pottery** and glass.

69 Tm Thulium

State: **Solid**
−69 +69 ◯100 Discovery: 1879

Laboratory sample of pure thulium

This machine emits X-rays using a very small amount of thulium.

Portable X-ray machine

This soft metal glows blue under ultraviolet (UV) light.

Thulium is the least abundant of all the lanthanide metals. It is used to create lasers that surgeons use to cut away damaged body tissue. Thulium also has a radioactive form that can produce X-rays; **portable X-ray machines** make use of this form.

70 Yb Ytterbium

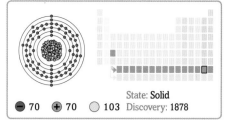

State: **Solid**
⊖ 70   ⊕ 70   ○ 103   Discovery: 1878

Ytterbium tends to be more reactive than other lanthanide metals. It is stored in sealed containers to stop the metal from reacting with oxygen. The **pure metal** has only a few uses. A small amount of ytterbium is used in making steel, while its compounds are used in some **lasers**.

Laser cutting

An ytterbium laser can cut through metals and plastics.

This bright, shiny metal can be hammered into thin sheets.

Laboratory sample of pure ytterbium

71 Lu Lutetium

Laboratory sample of pure lutetium

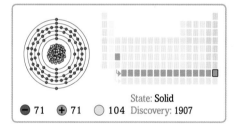

State: **Solid**
⊖ 71   ⊕ 71   ○ 104   Discovery: 1907

Some oil refineries use lutetium to break down crude oil to make fuels, such as gasoline and diesel.

This element is the hardest and densest lanthanide metal.

Lutetium was the last of the rare earth metals to be discovered. It is also the final member of the lanthanides. In its **pure form**, lutetium is very reactive and catches fire easily. It is rare and has few uses, mainly as a substance mixed with crude **oil**.

Oil refinery

117

This uranium (U) sample is waste material from a nuclear power plant.

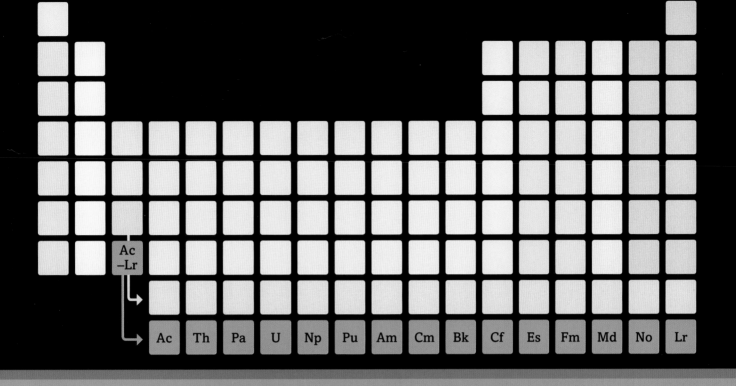

| Ac | Th | Pa | U | Np | Pu | Am | Cm | Bk | Cf | Es | Fm | Md | No | Lr |

Actinides

These metals are named after actinium (Ac), the first member of the group. Although this group is often shown as the bottom row in the periodic table to save space, they actually sit between radium (Ra), an alkali earth metal, and Rutherfodium (Rf), a transition metal. All the elements in this group are radioactive, and the final nine members are artificially produced in laboratories.

Atomic structure
All the elements in this group have two electrons in their outer shell. Their atoms all have seven electron shells.

Physical properties
Natural actinides are dense metals with high melting points. The physical properties of most of the artificial ones are unknown.

Chemical properties
The actinides are reactive metals and are never found in pure form in nature. They react easily with air, the halogens, and sulfur (S),

Compounds
Actinides form colorful compounds with halogens. Most actinide ores also contain compounds of oxygen (O) called oxides.

89
Ac Actinium

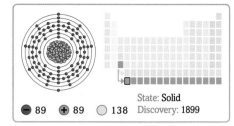

State: Solid
● 89 ⊕ 89 ○ 138 Discovery: 1899

Autunite

This radioactive mineral glows brightly in ultraviolet light.

Uraninite

This ore contains uranium, which breaks down into actinium.

This device uses radioactive actinium to measure the amount of water.

Neutron probe

Rare in nature, actinium is a metal formed by the decay of other radioactive elements. Its atoms are unstable and break down to make the elements francium and radon. Actinium is found in tiny amounts in uranium ores, such as **uraninite**, and has limited applications. Its isotopes are used in radiation therapy to treat cancer.

90
Th Thorium

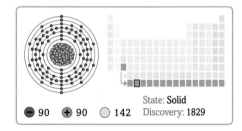

State: Solid
● 90 ⊕ 90 ○ 142 Discovery: 1829

Monazite

The most common natural radioactive metal, thorium is used inside vacuum tubes to allow an electric current to flow. It can also undergo nuclear fission, a process in which atoms split in two and release energy. Scientists are exploring ways of making thorium-powered nuclear reactors that produce electricity.

This durable rock made of solidified lava contains 12% thorium.

This thorium coating creates an electric current by releasing electrons.

This ore contains small crystals of thorium compounds.

Thorianite

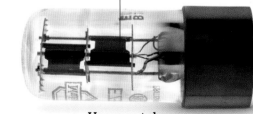

Vacuum tube

91 Pa Protactinium

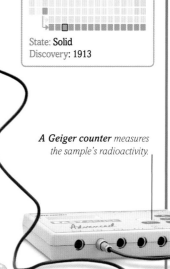

- 91 + 91 ○ 140

State: **Solid**
Discovery: **1913**

This vibrant green radioactive mineral contains tiny amounts of protactinium.

A Geiger counter measures the sample's radioactivity.

This bottle contains a protactinium sample.

Protactinium research

This brittle, shiny ore feels waxy.

The name protactinium means "before actinium." This is because a uranium atom decays to form a protactinium atom, which then quickly breaks down into an actinium atom. Small quantities of protactinium are found in ancient sands and mud. Geologists use Geiger counters to carry out **research** to calculate how old the sands are.

These used nuclear fuel rods contain protactinium.

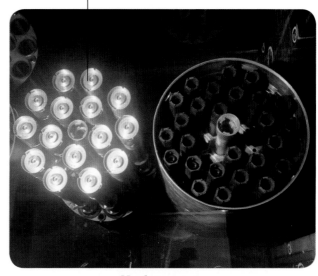

Torbernite

Nuclear waste

92
U Uranium

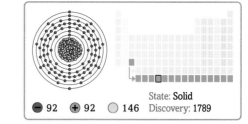

State: Solid
● 92 ⊕ 92 ○ 146 Discovery: 1789

Named after the planet Uranus, uranium was the first known radioactive element. In the early 20th century, some manufacturers used uranium in **glass bowl** glazes, only to realize later that it was a harmful metal. An unstable form, called uranium-235, is used as fuel in nuclear reactors and in atomic bombs.

These black sections contain uranium dioxide, which is the main source of uranium.

Chunk of pure uranium

Uraninite

This sample of pure uranium is waste from a nuclear plant.

Uranium mixed into glass makes this bowl glow bright green under ultraviolet (UV) lamps.

Glass bowl

93
Np Neptunium

State: Solid
● 93 ⊕ 93 ○ 144 Discovery: 1940

The radioactive elements in this mineral decay to form neptunium.

Uraninite

This cyclotron, built in 1938, was used to discover neptunium.

Cyclotron at the University of California, Berkeley

Sitting next to uranium in the periodic table, neptunium was named after the planet Neptune. It exists in small amounts in radioactive ores, such as aeschynite. It forms during nuclear explosions and was first identified inside a machine called a **cyclotron**. There are no known uses for neptunium.

94
Pu Plutonium

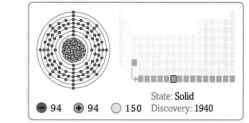

State: **Solid**
● 94   ⊕ 94   ○ 150   Discovery: 1940

Uraninite

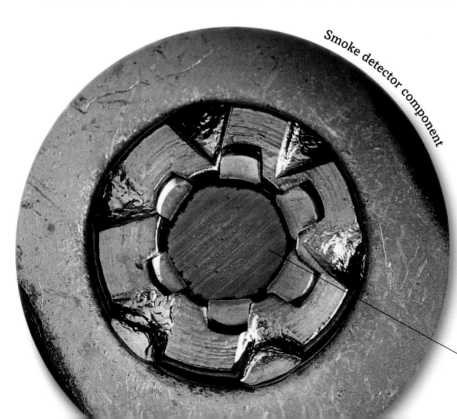

This Martian rover uses the heat given off by a supply of plutonium to generate electrical power.

Hardly any plutonium exists in nature: most of it has decayed into other elements over time. It was discovered during the development of nuclear bombs in World War II. Today, plutonium is used mostly as a nuclear fuel.

This ore *contains trace amounts of plutonium.*

This plutonium battery *was used in early pacemakers.*

1970's pacemaker battery

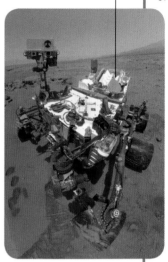

Curiosity Rover

95
Am Americium

State: **Solid**
● 95   ⊕ 95   ○ 148   Discovery: 1944

Smoke detector component

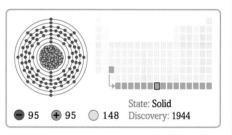

This metallic element is not found in nature. Instead, it is produced inside nuclear reactors when uranium or plutonium atoms are bombarded with neutrons. Remarkably, americium is the most common radioactive element used in the home. Radioactivity emitted by americium atoms causes the air inside **smoke detectors** to conduct electricity. When smoke disrupts the electric current, an alarm goes off.

This smoke detector *contains tiny, harmless quantities of americium.*

123

96
Cm Curium

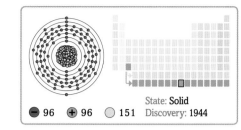

State: **Solid**
- 96 + 96 ○ 151 Discovery: 1944

This lander studied the surface composition of the comet 67P.

Philae lander

Marie Curie working in her laboratory

Curium is a silvery, radioactive metal that glows reddish purple in the dark. This element was discovered by the scientist Glenn T. Seaborg at the University of California, Berkeley. It was named after **Marie Curie**, the scientist who discovered the element polonium. Several space probes, such as the **Philae comet lander**, use X-ray devices containing curium to study their environment.

97
Bk Berkelium

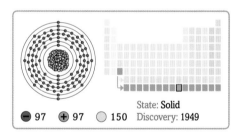

State: **Solid**
- 97 + 97 ○ 150 Discovery: 1949

This element was named after the city of Berkeley—home to the University of California laboratory where this artificial element was discovered. It was first synthesized by **Glenn T. Seaborg**. Berkelium has no uses other than the creation of heavier elements, such as tennessine.

Seaborg helped develop the atom bomb, but **opposed using it** in World War II.

University of California, Berkeley campus

Glenn T. Seaborg

98 Cf Californium

● 98 ⊕ 98 ○ 153

State: **Solid**
Discovery: 1950

Water detector

This machine uses californium to find water underground.

Pellets of radioactive californium

This isotope, or form, of californium produces a lot of neutrons.

Californium is named after the state of California. This soft, silvery metal does not exist in nature and is made by smashing berkelium atoms with neutrons in a particle accelerator (a machine in which atoms are smashed together). This **radioactive element** is used in the treatment of cancer.

99 Es Einsteinium

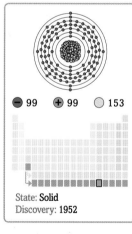

● 99 ⊕ 99 ○ 153

State: **Solid**
Discovery: 1952

Albert Einstein in his study

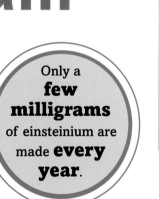

Only a **few milligrams** of einsteinium are made **every year**.

Einsteinium was discovered in the chemicals left over after the first hydrogen bomb test in 1952. The huge explosion fused smaller atoms together to make larger ones, including einsteinium. This element was named after the great German-born scientist **Albert Einstein**, and was found to be a silvery, radioactive metal that glows blue in the dark. It is only used for making heavier elements, such as mendelevium.

125

100 Fm Fermium

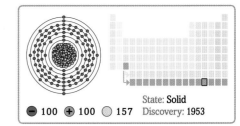

State: **Solid**
● 100 ⊕ 100 ○ 157 Discovery: 1953

This artificial element was named after the Italian scientist Enrico Fermi. He built the first nuclear reactor in 1942, starting the American effort to build nuclear weapons during World War II. Fermium was first identified in the debris of an atom bomb test in 1953. This unstable element has no known uses beyond research.

Some scientists call Enrico Fermi the "father of the **atomic age.**"

Enrico Fermi

101 Md Mendelevium

● 101 ⊕ 101 ○ 157

State: **Solid**
Discovery: **1955**

Mendeleev's periodic table

Mendeleev's notes from 1869 show his method of arranging elements in columns and rows.

Dmitri Mendeleev

Mendelevium is named after the Russian chemist Dmitri Mendeleev, who invented the periodic table. Mendelevium is produced in very small amounts by firing parts of helium atoms at einsteinium atoms in a particle accelerator (a machine in which atoms are smashed together).

102 No Nobelium

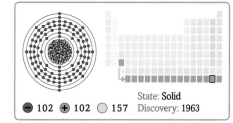

State: Solid
● 102 ⊕ 102 ○ 157 Discovery: 1963

This artificial metal is named after the Swedish chemist Alfred Nobel, who created the Nobel Prizes in his will. It was discovered in 1963 by a team of scientists working in California. This team included **Albert Ghiorso**, **Torbjørn Sikkeland**, and **John R. Walton**. They used a particle accelerator to fire carbon atoms at curium atoms, creating nobelium atoms, which broke apart within minutes.

Albert Ghiorso, Torbjørn Sikkeland, and John R. Walton

103 Lr Lawrencium

An early cyclotron

Lawrencium was produced at the **Berkeley lab** set up by Ernest Lawrence.

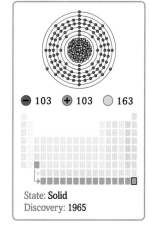

● 103 ⊕ 103 ○ 163

State: Solid
Discovery: 1965

Lawrencium is named after the US scientist Ernest Lawrence, who developed the first cyclotron particle accelerator. This is a machine in which parts of atoms are smashed together by making them spin around in circles. Lawrencium atoms were produced in a similar machine by firing boron atoms at californium atoms.

Pure gallium (Ga)
becomes liquid
at 84.2°F (29°C).

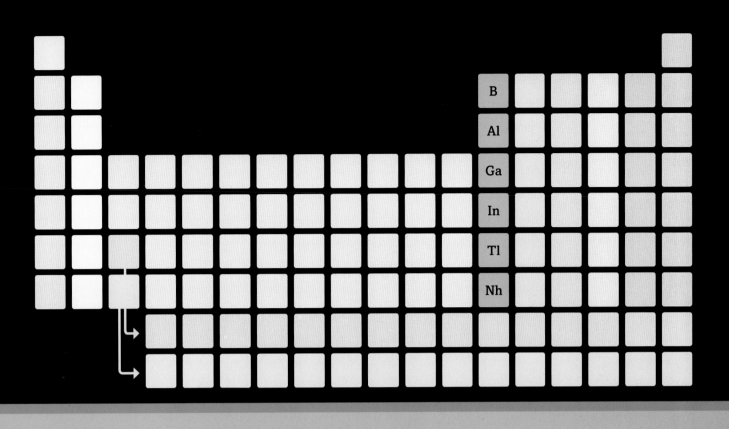

The Boron Group

This group contains five natural elements and one artificial element called nihonium (Nh). Although these elements are not very reactive, none of them is found in a pure form in nature. Boron (B), the first member, is a semimetal (an element that has properties of both metals and nonmetals), while the rest are metals. The second member, aluminum (Al), is the most common metal in Earth's rocks.

Atomic structure
Members of this group have three electrons in the outer shell of every atom. Some elements have unstable isotopes.

Physical properties
All elements, except boron, are shiny solids. Every member of this group is soft, except for boron (B), which is one of the hardest elements.

Chemical properties
Most of these elements don't react with water but can react with oxygen to form oxides. In air, aluminum develops a thin coat of oxide that protects it.

Compounds
They form compounds by losing electrons to other elements. All of them react with oxygen (O) by bonding to three oxygen atoms.

5
B Boron

State: **Solid**
Discovery: 1808
⊖ 5 ⊕ 5 ◯ 6

Forms

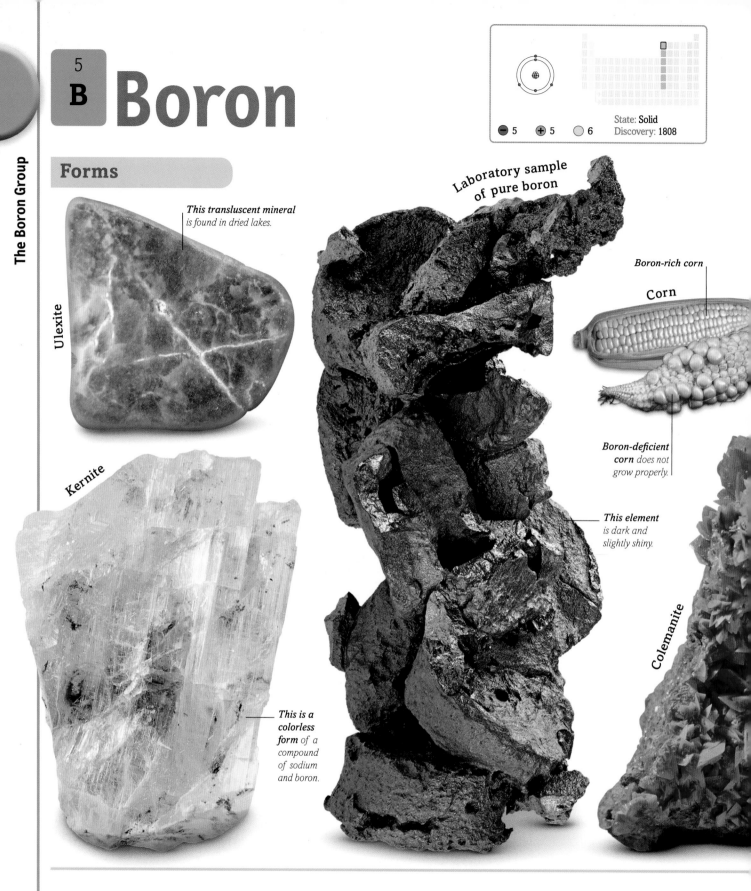

This transluscent mineral is found in dried lakes.

Ulexite

Kernite

This is a colorless form of a compound of sodium and boron.

Laboratory sample of pure boron

Boron-rich corn

Corn

Boron-deficient corn does not grow properly.

This element is dark and slightly shiny.

Colemanite

Some boron compounds are among the toughest artificial substances on Earth, with only diamond being harder. This element is a very hard material and becomes even harder when made to react with carbon or nitrogen. **Pure boron** can be extracted from various minerals, including **ulexite** and **kernite**. The demand for this element was once so high that people moved to live in the extreme heat of **Death Valley, California**, to work in boron mines there. Compounds of boron in soil are essential for plants to grow healthily. We use boron in our

This searing desert is one of the main places on Earth where boron is found.

Death Valley, California

Needle- and leaf-shaped crystals

Uses

This tough glass contains boron oxide.

Measuring cup

Boric acid

These white crystals are obtained from sodium borate.

👓 THÉNARD AND GAY-LUSSAC

The salt sodium borate, also called borax, was already in use 1,000 years ago. In 1808, the Frenchmen Joseph Louis Gay-Lussac and Louis Jacques Thénard isolated pure boron by heating borax with potassium.

Louis Jacques Thénard
Born into a poor family, Thénard excelled as a scientist. He also discovered a compound called hydrogen peroxide.

Joseph Louis Gay-Lussac
This French chemist is also remembered for discovering that the pressure of a gas goes up with its temperature.

This clay is bouncy but also firm because it contains boron.

Modeling clay

LCD screen

This screen is composed of boron-rich glass, which makes it scratch-resistant.

Boron carbide is one of the **hardest** materials in use today.

The protective body of this tank contains boron carbide, a compound of boron and carbon.

Military tank

homes every day. Tough, heat-resistant glassware, such as **measuring cups**, are strengthened with boron. **Boric acid** is a natural antiseptic and can be used to treat minor cuts and scrapes. A flexible layer of boron-based fiberglass is used to toughen thin **LCD screens** for televisions and laptops. Even some kinds of **modeling clay** and bouncy silly putty contain boron compounds. Boron is named after a crumbly white salt called borax, which is used in detergents. The element is also present in a diverse range of objects, from insecticides to armor for **military tanks**.

Aluminum

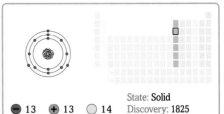

Forms

Variscite

Alum crystal

This crystal contains aluminum and sulfur compounds.

This aluminum ore is the world's main source of the element.

Bauxite

Pellets of pure aluminum refined in a laboratory

This slice of aluminum phosphate mineral has a turquoise-green color.

Reflective surface

Although aluminum is the most common metal in Earth's rocks, scientists did not discover it until the early 1800s. Even then, it took a further 80 years for scientists to work out how to use the ore **bauxite** to extract large amounts of **pure aluminum**. It can also be found in other minerals, including **variscite**. Today, aluminum is often recycled because producing it from scratch requires 15 times more energy. The metal makes a strong, shiny **foil** when rolled flat, and is useful for storing foods. A **fire protection suit** made

Uses

Tennis racket

This aluminum frame makes the racket light.

This foil does not break even as it is bent and twisted.

Aluminum foil

This suit protects against temperatures up to 1,800°F (1,000°C).

Aluminum can

This can is produced from recycled aluminum.

Fire protection suit

RECYCLING ALUMINUM

Aluminum is expensive to purify, so it is often recycled instead. Soda cans are almost 100 percent pure aluminum and can be shredded, melted down, and made into new cans.

1. Used cans are collected for processing.

2. They are crushed into small bricks.

3. The blocks are shredded into tiny pieces.

4. The pieces are then melted into large blocks.

5. The blocks are then cast into smaller sections.

6. These are pressed into metal sheets.

7. New cans are made from these sheets.

Smartwatch

Parts of this dome are made of aluminum.

Recycling one aluminum can saves enough energy to run a TV for three hours.

Esplanade Theatre, Singapore

Aluminum cables are lightweight.

The aluminum casing protects the touchscreen.

Overhead cables

This plane's fuselage is built from sheets of aluminum stretched around a frame.

Boeing 737

from this foil reflects away heat. Aluminum is the most widely used metal after iron. It is very lightweight compared to iron's alloy steel and almost as strong. A dome made from aluminum, such as the one in the **Esplanade Theatre** in Singapore, can be much larger than a steel-based one, which would collapse under its own weight. Aluminum is also a good electrical conductor and so is used in **overhead cables**. Tough aluminum alloys are used to produce parts of some aircraft, including the **Boeing 737**.

JET TURBINE
The curved blades of this jet engine are shaped very precisely to catch the air, and they are also strong enough to stay stiff when working at high temperatures. There are several tough metals that fit these requirements, but most are very dense, making them too heavy for an engine powering an airplane into the air. That leaves only one metal for the job: aluminum.

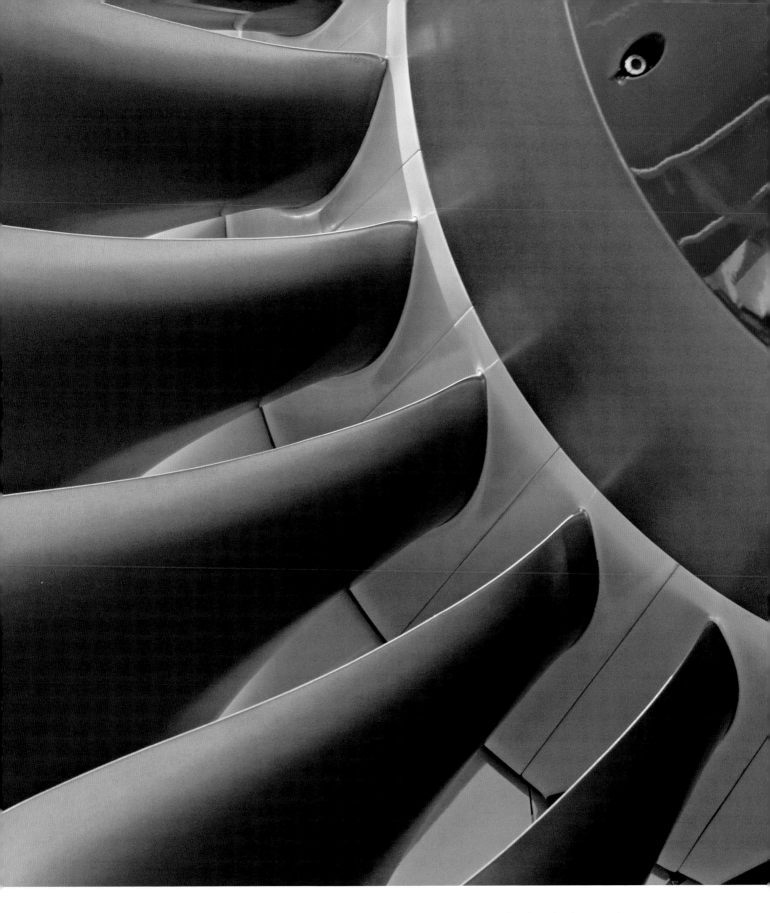

Aluminum is what makes high-speed, long-range air travel possible. Easily molded, it is one-quarter the weight of steel, and it never rusts. Steel is stronger, but a plane made from it would be too heavy to fly. Instead aluminum is mixed with titanium and steel to produce tough yet lightweight alloys, which are used in the engines and bodies of jet aircraft. There is almost twice as much aluminum in Earth's rock as there is iron. However, purifying aluminum takes a lot of energy. Once pure, though, it can be recycled over and over again. So, one day these engine blades might transform into a soda can.

31 Ga Gallium

State: **Solid**
Discovery: 1875
⊖ 31 ⊕ 31 ◯ 39

Forms

Diaspore

The needlelike crystals form on the surface.

Pure gallium has a very low melting point.

Cube of melting gallium

Uses

Thermometer

This medical thermometer uses a gallium alloy instead of mercury.

A gallium laser is used to read Blu-ray disks.

Blu-ray disk

Red LED lights

The red LED gets its color from gallium compounds.

Opportunity rover

The solar panels powering this rover, which is exploring Mars, contain gallium and arsenic.

Gallium melts at just 84.2°F (29°C), which means it soon becomes liquid when held in the hand. This element is found in small amounts in ores of zinc and aluminum, such as **diaspore**. **Pure gallium** is isolated when the other elements from this ore are extracted.

Gallium has a number of uses. It is mixed with indium and tin to form a liquid alloy called galinstan, which can be used in **thermometers**. Gallium is also found in **Blu-ray lasers**, **LEDs**, and some solar panels, such as those on NASA's Mars **rovers**.

49 In Indium

State: **Solid**
Discovery: 1863
● 49   ⊕ 49   ○ 66

Forms

Sphalerite

When bent, indium produces a **"tin cry"**—a sound similar to a **scream**.

Pure indium mold cast in a laboratory

This zinc mineral *is the main source of indium.*

Pure indium *is soft enough to draw lines on paper.*

Uses

This touchscreen *has a grid of very thin, transparent wires made of indium tin oxide.*

Touchscreen tablet

Welder's goggles

Protective goggles *coated with indium stop the heat damaging the welder's eyes.*

Transistor

The tiny electronic switches *inside this transistor contain indium.*

This glass coated with indium oxide is shiny but still lets light through.

Windows in a building

Indium is named after indigo, which is the color of the light its atoms release when electrified. Its minerals are rare, and most of the metal is obtained from lead and zinc ores, such as **sphalerite**. **Pure indium** is very soft, and the element is mostly used in compound form. For example, a compound called indium tin oxide used on a **touchscreen** allows the computer to detect when a finger makes contact with the screen. Indium is also required in microchips, and to produce **welder's goggles** and **windows** that are heat- and glare-proof.

81
Tl Thallium

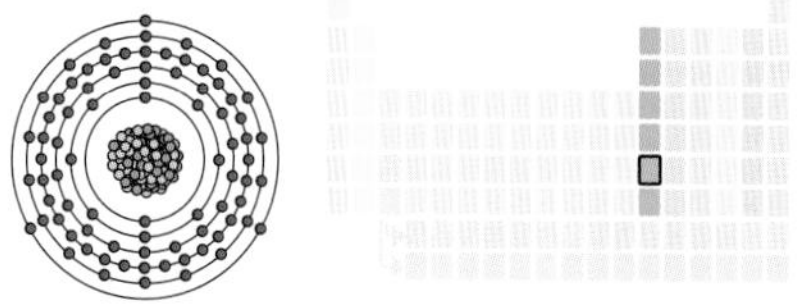

State: **Solid**
- 81 + 81 ○ 123 Discovery: 1861

Forms

This mineral contains aluminum sulfate (alum) with several different metals, including thallium.

Alum mineral

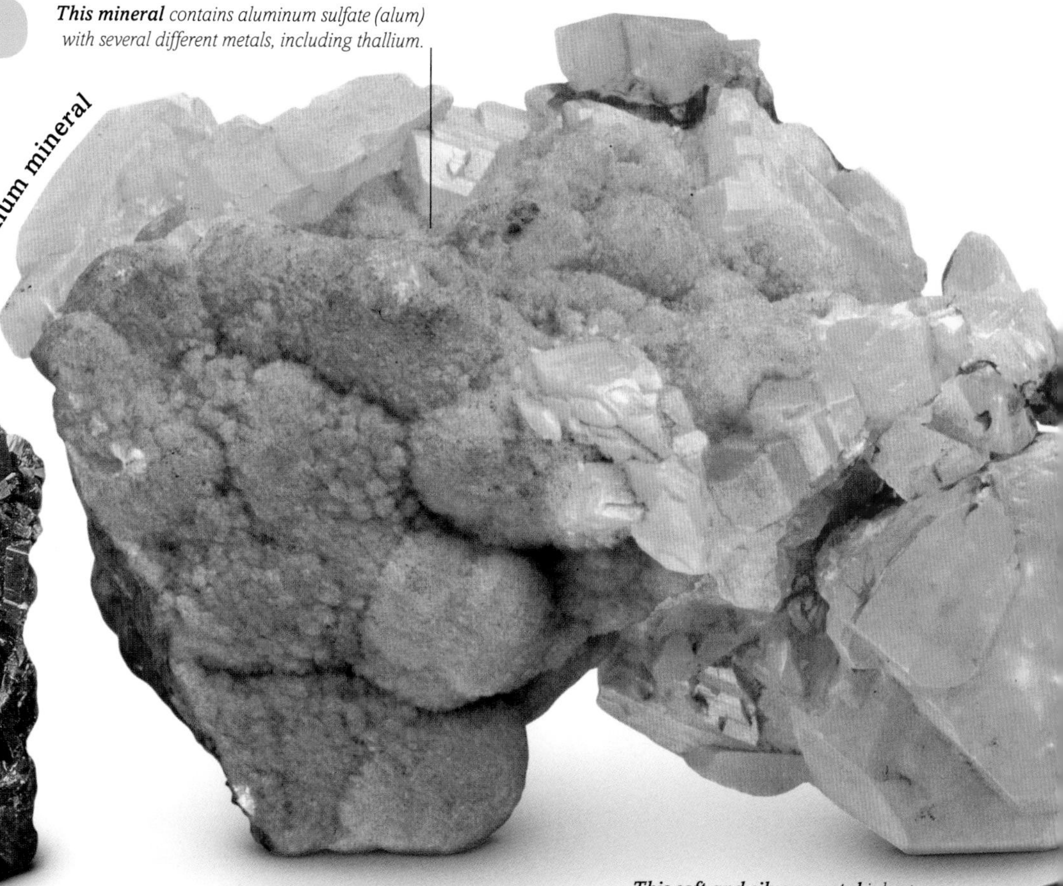

This mineral contains iron, sulfur, and tiny amounts of thallium.

Pyrite

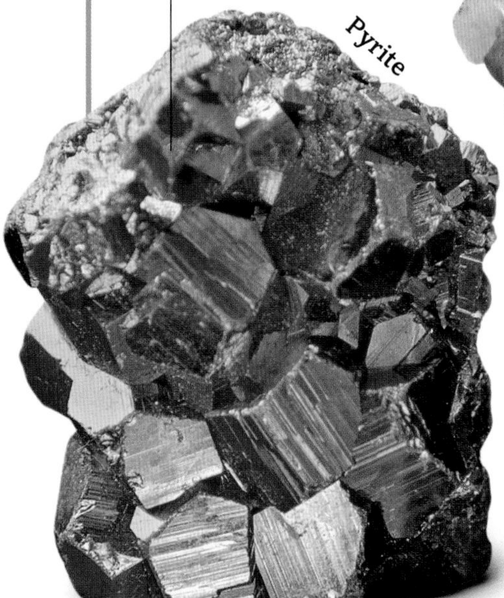

This soft and silvery metal is kept in a sealed glass tube because it is highly toxic and reacts easily with air.

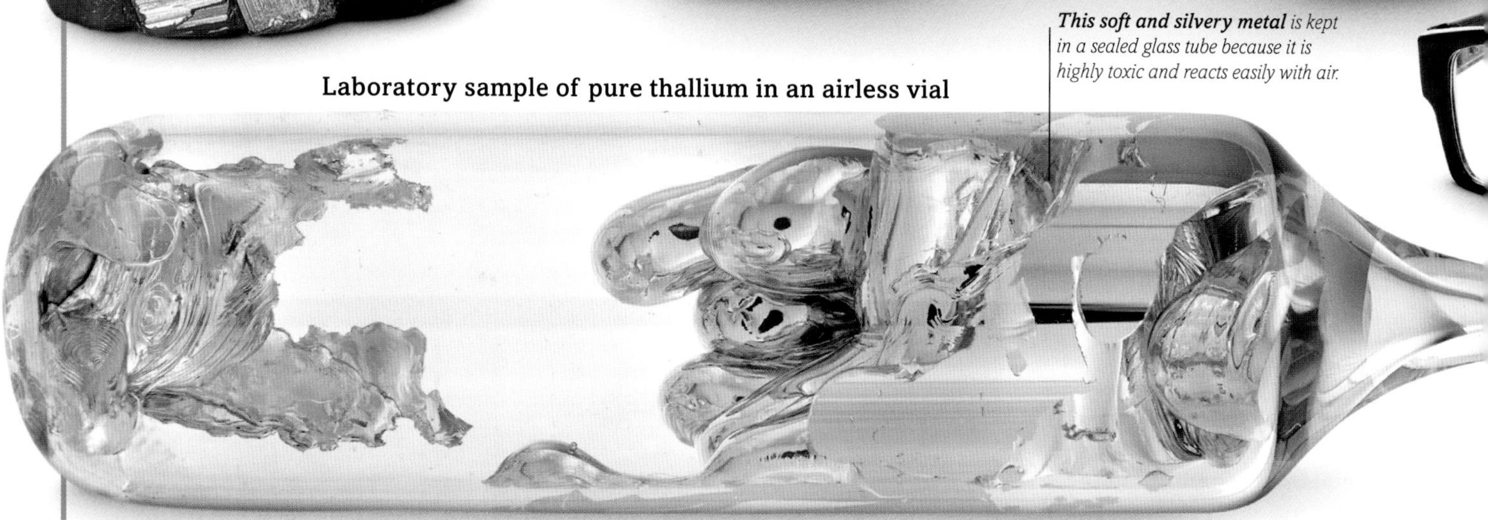

Laboratory sample of pure thallium in an airless vial

Thallium was named after the Greek word *thallos*, which means "green shoot": it was first identified from the colors in its flame, which includes a bright green light. Thallium was discovered in 1861 by William Crookes and Claude-Auguste Lamy. Although both chemists worked separately, they found the element in the same way—as a residue while making strong acids using the mineral **pyrite**. Thallium is also found in **alum minerals**, but most thallium extracted is a by-product of the extraction of copper or lead. **Pure thallium** is

Uses

Heart function scan

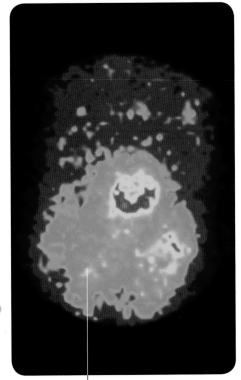

Blood injected with a thallium compound shows on a patient's heart scan.

Eyeglasses

Until the 1970s, thallium salts were commonly used as **ant poison**.

These thin lenses contain strong, thallium-infused glass.

toxic and has to be handled with care when used. A chlorine compound of thallium is used in **scans** to study a patient's blood circulation. Thallium oxide also helps make glass stronger for use in **eyeglasses** and cameras.

113 Nh Nihonium

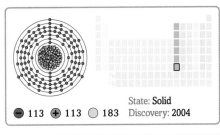

State: **Solid**
⊖ 113 ⊕ 113 ◯ 183 Discovery: 2004

Kozuka Morita (left), with a visiting official at the RIKEN Nuclear Research Center, Wako, Japan

Nihonium was named after the Japanese word *nihon*, which means Japan. A metallic element, nihonium was first detected in 2003 by teams studying the artificial element moscovium, which has the atomic number of 115. They noticed that atoms of moscovium broke apart after only a few seconds into atoms of an element with an atomic number of 113. In 2004, Kozuka Morita and a team of scientists at the **RIKEN Nuclear Research Center** in Japan isolated this element in a different way: they fused bismuth and zinc atoms together.

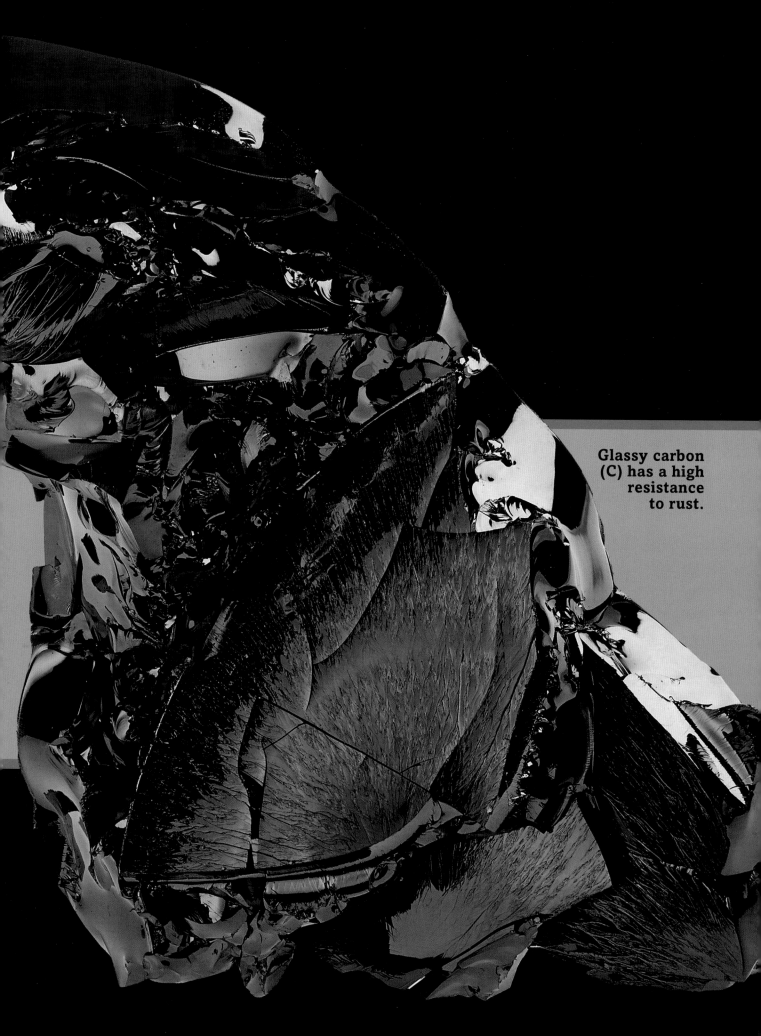

Glassy carbon
(C) has a high
resistance
to rust.

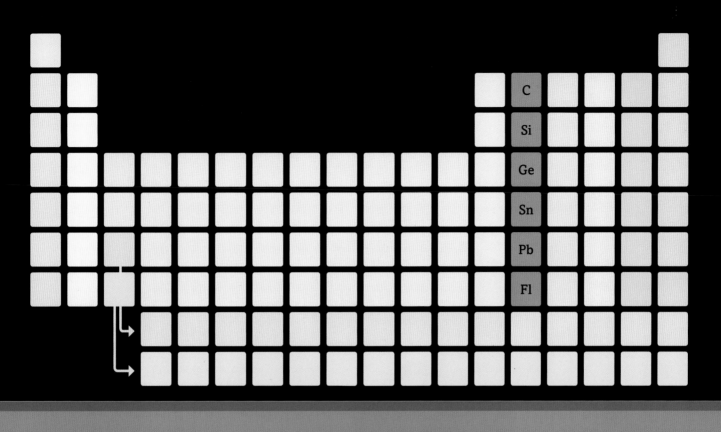

The Carbon Group

This group contains one nonmetal, two semimetals, and three metals. The nonmetal carbon (C) is the main element in all living things. The semimetals—silicon (Si) and germanium (Ge)—are elements that have the properties of both metals and nonmetals, and they are essential in electronics. Two of the metals—tin (Sn) and lead (Pb)—have been used by humans for centuries. Flerovium (Fl), an artificial element, has no known uses.

Atomic structure
Members of this group have four electrons in the outer shell of each atom. These atoms can bond with up to four other atoms.

Physical properties
At room temperature, all natural elements in this set are solid. Flerovium (Fl) is an artificial element, and scientists think it may be a solid.

Chemical properties
All natural elements in this group can react with hydrogen (H). Carbon (C) and silicon (Si) can react with both metals and nonmetals.

Compounds
These elements react with hydrogen to form compounds called hydrides. Each element can lose up to four electrons when forming compounds.

Carbon

Forms

This compressed form of sooty carbon is formed underground.

Coal

Glassy carbon

Glossy surface

Crude oil

Mixture *of liquid, carbon-rich compounds*

Raw diamond

This colorless crystal forms in magma deep underground.

This diamond's brightness depends on its cut, which determines how many times light entering the gem will reflect inside.

The shiny, metallic surface feels soft and slippery.

Laboratory sample of graphite

Cut diamond

Carbon has the largest number of compounds of any element—with more than nine million known. Carbon is the fourth most common element in the universe. Each carbon atom can bond to four others, allowing them to form chains and rings. Pure carbon exists in three forms on Earth—**graphite**, **diamond**, and buckminsterfullerene (a structure based on 60 interlinked carbon atoms). Diamond is the hardest substance in nature. It is often used in jewelry. The blades of some **saws** are coated with diamonds, and

Uses

Diamond blade saw

This sharp blade is coated with tiny diamonds.

Water purifier filter

This carbon filter absorbs harmful chemicals in water.

Battery

This battery has a graphite core that carries electric current.

Carbon-fiber bicycle

Sturdy and lightweight frame

LOTUS Sport

This **strong** but **light** frame is made by fusing carbon fibers.

This wheel is composed of carbon fiber and some other materials, which make it rigid.

This flame is fueled by carbon-rich oil.

Kerosene lamp

Soft graphite leaves a mark when pressed against paper.

Pencil "lead" containing graphite, not lead

This flexible plastic material is composed of chains of carbon and hydrogen atoms.

Polyethylene bag

HARD AND SOFT CARBON

Diamond and graphite have different properties because of the arrangement of their atoms—tetrahedrons in diamond, and sheets of hexagons in graphite.

Hard as diamond
The tetrahedron, or pyramid structure, of atoms creates a rigid shape that is equally strong in all directions.

Soft as graphite
Graphite contains layers of carbon atoms that slide over each other easily because the forces between them are weak.

can cut into anything. Only a diamond can cut another diamond. Graphite is much softer, which is why it is used in **pencil "lead."** It is also used in some batteries. Coal is currently the largest source of fuel for the generation of electricity, but its fumes are also known to have harmful environmental and health effects. Crude oil, natural gas, and **coal** are hydrocarbons (compounds containing only hydrogen and carbon) that occur in nature. They can be used as fuels and as plastics for objects such as **polyethylene bags**.

PINK DIAMOND
With a mass of only just over 0.1 oz (3 g), this jewel—known as The Sweet Josephine—is one of the largest pink diamonds ever sold. Diamonds are normally colorless forms of pure carbon, and if there is any color, it comes from tiny amounts of another substance. For example, boron makes the gem appear blue. Strangely, pink diamonds have no impurities, and no one knows why they are pink.

The Sweet Josephine was cut from raw diamond that is more than 1.5 billion years old. This formed 93 miles (150 km) beneath Earth's surface and was then pushed up by a volcanic eruption, before eventually being dug out at a mine in Australia. Diamonds form when carbon is squeezed and heated to more than 1,832°F (1,000°C). This process rearranges the carbon atoms into a rigid crystal that makes diamond the world's hardest substance. The process also gives diamond the ability to bend light, a property that gives these jewels their glorious sparkle. With the right cut and polish, a diamond can be made into a beautiful gem that is prized throughout the world.

14
Si Silicon

State: **Solid**
Discovery: 1824

⊖ 14   ⊕ 14   ◯ 14

Forms

Amethyst

Fulgurite

Laboratory sample of pure silicon

This glassy mineral tube *is formed when quartz-rich sand is struck by lightning.*

The pure element *can shatter easily.*

Tiny hairs on these leaves *have silica tips that break off when you touch them, releasing chemicals that sting.*

Stinging nettle

Sand

Sand *is mostly tiny grains of quartz that have broken away from rocks.*

This purple form of quartz *gets its color from iron impurities.*

About 90 percent of the minerals that make up Earth's rocks contain silicon, a common element in our planet's crust. Nearly all silicon minerals are compounds of silicon and oxygen, known as silicates. The most common silicate is quartz, the mineral form of silicon dioxide, or silica. It is also the most common substance in **sand**. **Amethyst** is a type of quartz. Quartz deposits are widely found in rocks such as granite and sandstone. A valuable type of silica is **opal**, which is used as a gemstone. The clays used to make pottery and **ceramics** are also silicates.

Uses

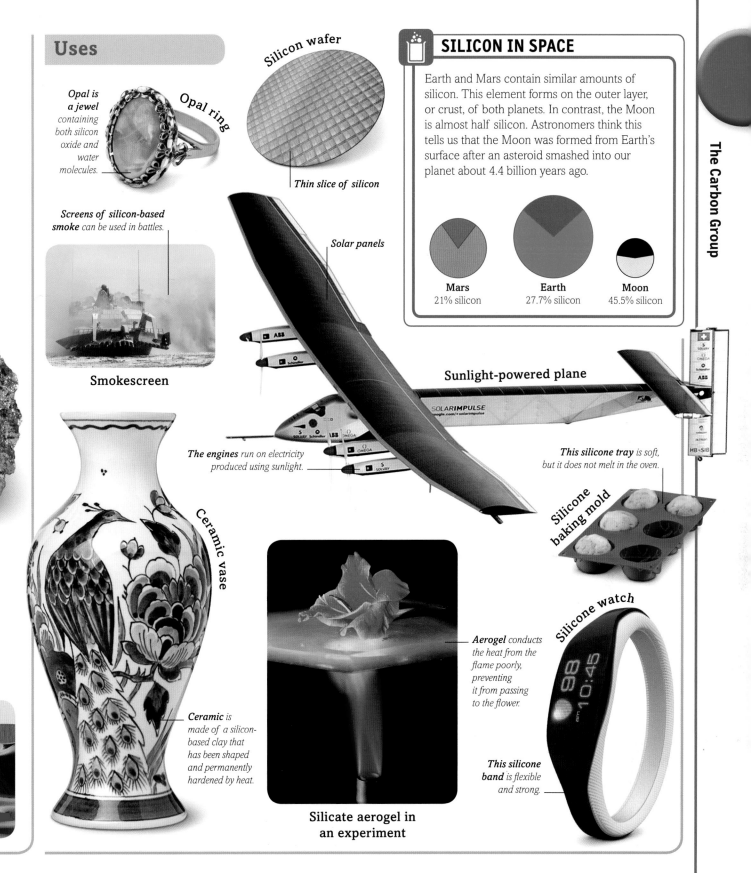

Opal is a jewel containing both silicon oxide and water molecules.

Opal ring

Silicon wafer

Thin slice of silicon

Screens of silicon-based smoke can be used in battles.

Smokescreen

Solar panels

The engines run on electricity produced using sunlight.

Sunlight-powered plane

Ceramic vase

Ceramic is made of a silicon-based clay that has been shaped and permanently hardened by heat.

Aerogel conducts the heat from the flame poorly, preventing it from passing to the flower.

Silicate aerogel in an experiment

This silicone tray is soft, but it does not melt in the oven.

Silicone baking mold

Silicone watch

This silicone band is flexible and strong.

SILICON IN SPACE

Earth and Mars contain similar amounts of silicon. This element forms on the outer layer, or crust, of both planets. In contrast, the Moon is almost half silicon. Astronomers think this tells us that the Moon was formed from Earth's surface after an asteroid smashed into our planet about 4.4 billion years ago.

Mars
21% silicon

Earth
27.7% silicon

Moon
45.5% silicon

One of the most important uses of silicon is in electronics. Thin slices called **silicon wafers** drive electronic circuits. This versatile element is also used to turn sunlight into electricity in solar panels. Artificial silica is used to create **aerogel**, a lightweight but tough substance that does not conduct heat well. It is used in firefighting suits, and prevents flames reaching a firefighter. Another silicon compound is silicone, which can be molded into any shape, and is used in a wide range of products from **baking molds** to **watches**.

32
Ge Germanium

● 32 ＋ 32 ○ 41

State: **Solid**
Discovery: 1886

Forms

Germanite

This sulfur mineral is rich in germanium.

The pure form is shiny like a metal, but brittle.

Disk of pure germanium refined in a laboratory

Uses

Camera lens

The germanium oxide in the glass of this lens bends surrounding light from a large area into the camera.

This microchip is made of silicon and germanium.

Smartphone microchip

Germanium is found in the **atmosphere** of **Jupiter**.

This car contains a germanium-based sensor that measures its distance from obstacles.

Car with germanium sensor

This semimetal is named after the country Germany. It was discovered there in 1886 by chemist Clemens A. Winkler, nearly 20 years after Russian chemist Dmitri Mendeleev predicted its existence and properties. **Germanite** is a mineral rich in germanium, but this element is mainly extracted from the ores of silver, copper, and lead. One of its compounds, germanium oxide, is used in wide-angle **camera lenses**. It is also used in some **microchips** and in a number of **car sensors** that aid in navigation.

50 Sn Tin

- 50 + 50 ○ 69
State: **Solid**
Discovery: **c. 2100** BCE

Forms

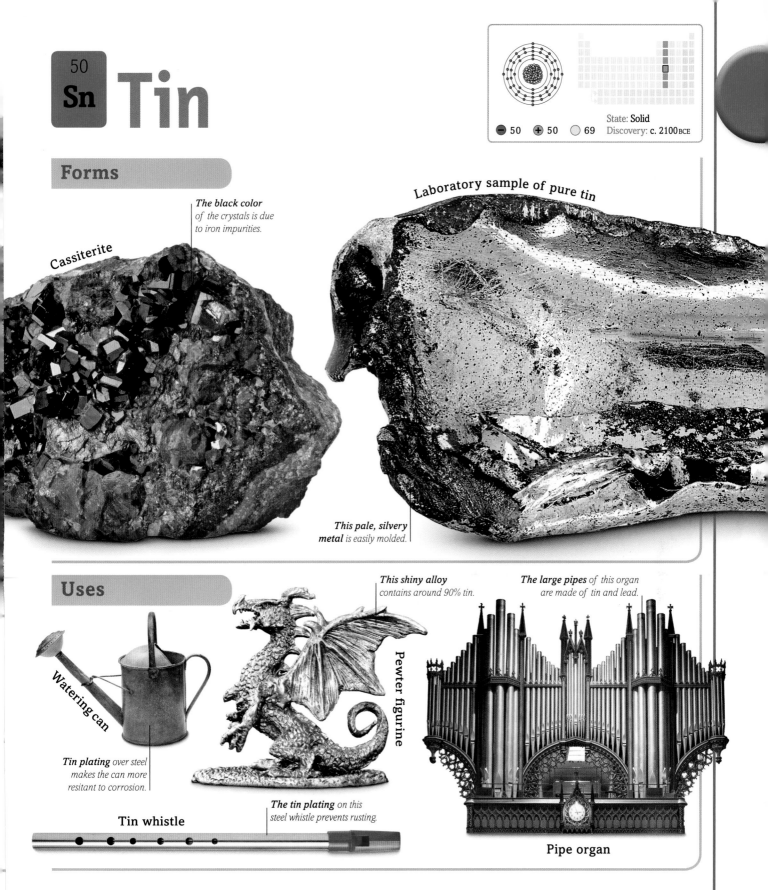

Cassiterite

The black color of the crystals is due to iron impurities.

Laboratory sample of pure tin

This pale, silvery metal is easily molded.

Uses

Watering can

Tin plating over steel makes the can more resitant to corrosion.

Tin whistle

The tin plating on this steel whistle prevents rusting.

This shiny alloy contains around 90% tin.

Pewter figurine

The large pipes of this organ are made of tin and lead.

Pipe organ

Tin was one of the first metals used by humans. As long as 5,000 years ago, tin was mixed with copper to make bronze, an alloy that was stronger than either pure metal. The ore **cassiterite** is the main source of **pure tin**. Uses for tin are many, including plating steel objects, such as **cans**, to prevent them corroding. A compound called tin chloride is used for dyeing silks. This metal continues to be used in a variety of tough alloys, including **pewter**, soft solder, and bronze.

149

Molten bismuth (Bi) solidifies to form hopper crystals.

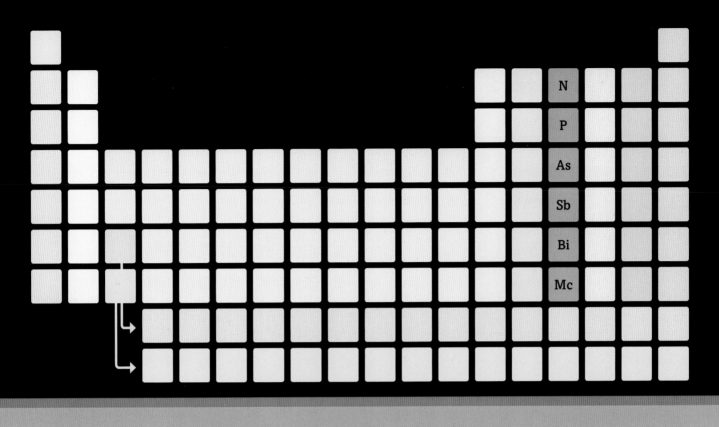

The Nitrogen Group

This group includes different types of natural element—nonmetals, semimetals, and dense metals—as well as moscovium (Mc), an artificial element. The group is also known as "pnictogens." This derives from the Greek word *pnigein*, which means "to choke" and refers to the potential toxicity of nitrogen (N) in certain forms.

Atomic structure
Members of this group have atoms with five electrons in the outer shell. These atoms can form up to three bonds at the same time.

Physical properties
All the members are solids, except nitrogen (N). The density of elements increases down the group: bismuth (Bi) is 8,000 times denser than nitrogen.

Chemical properties
Phosphorus (P), which exists in two main forms, is reactive, but the others in this group are fairly stable.

Compounds
When reacting with three hydrogen (H) atoms, all members of the group form reactive gaseous compounds called hydrides.

7 N Nitrogen

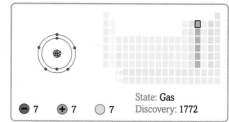

State: **Gas**
Discovery: 1772
⊖ 7   ⊕ 7   ◯ 7

Forms

Pure nitrogen in a glass sphere

Pure nitrogen gas is trapped inside this glass sphere.

Nitrogen gas gives off a purple glow when electrified.

Saturn's largest moon has an atmosphere containing 48% nitrogen.

Titan

Liquid nitrogen

This clear and colorless liquid forms when nitrogen is cooled to below −319°F (−195°C).

Nitratine

This is a naturally occurring form of sodium nitrate.

Bacteria living inside plant roots can take nitrogen from the air for use by the plant.

Microscopic image of root nodule

Nitrogen surrounds us all the time because it is the transparent gas that makes up nearly three-quarters of Earth's atmosphere. Since **pure nitrogen** does not react easily, its **liquid form** can be used to freeze and preserve items such as blood and tissue samples. **Nitratine** is one of the few minerals rich in nitrogen. Some useful nitrogen compounds can be made by industrial processes. A group of nitrogen compounds is used in explosives, including **TNT** and **nitroglycerine**. When ignited, they explode because the bonds between nitrogen atoms

Uses

Trinitrotoluene (TNT) does not explode below 464°F (240°C).

TNT

This lander used 12 hydrazine-powered thrusters to land on Mars.

Phoenix Mars Lander

Nitroglycerine can be used to treat heart conditions.

Nitroglycerine spray

Motorcycles use nitromethane to fuel their powerful engines.

Kawasaki ZX14

Drag bike

These nitrogen-based azo dyes are often used to color textiles.

Textile dye

Superstrong glues contain small nitrogen compounds that link together.

SUPER GLUE
NET WT. 0.11 OZ. (3g)

Super glue

These fertilizers contain compounds called ammonium nitrates that promote growth in plants.

Nitrogen fertilizer

NITROGEN CYCLE

Nitrogen is essential for life. The nitrogen cycle is a process that constantly recycles nitrogen between the Earth's atmopshere and all living things.

1. Lightning turns nitrogen in the air into nitrogen compounds, which dissolve in rainwater and fall to the ground.

5. Bacteria break apart nitrogen compounds in the soil, returning pure nitrogen into the air.

2. Bacteria in the soil and plant roots produce nitrogen compounds from pure nitrogen in the air.

3. Animals take in nitrogen compounds when they eat, and release it in their dung.

4. Fungi, such as mushrooms, break down dead plants and animals, which release their nitrogen compounds back into the soil.

atoms detach very quickly. Nitrogen fuels, such as nitromethane, are used in **drag bikes**, providing a lot more power than carbon-and-hydrogen-only fuels, such as gasoline. The compound hydrazine is used in thrusters on spacecraft, such as the **Phoenix Mars Lander**.

Some nitrogen compounds are put in **dyes** and **glues**. An industrial technique called the Haber process turns nitrogen and hydrogen gas into ammonia, a liquid commonly used to make **nitrogen fertilizers**. When mixed with soil, these fertilizers boost plant growth.

DRAG RACING
Zooming along a dead-straight track, these all-powerful dragsters accelerate all the way to the finish line. They contain massive engines filled with an extra-powerful fuel called nitromethane, which is often shortened to "nitro." Burning eight times faster than the regular gasoline used in most cars, this super fuel can push dragsters to speeds in excess of 300 mph (480 km/h).

Nitromethane contains carbon, hydrogen, and nitrogen, but it is the latter element that really gives this fuel its immense power. During the process of combustion—when oxygen is mixed with the fuel in the race car's mighty engine—nitromethane burns so violently that nitrogen escapes from the fuel and returns to its pure form. This chain of events leads to a release of energy, which propels the dragsters to breakneck speeds. Although these races are an incredible spectacle to behold, driving using nitromethane can be dangerous due to the explosive nature of nitrogen when used in this way: drag racers are taking a risk to win.

15 P Phosphorus

Forms

State: **Solid**
Discovery: **1669**

● 15 ➕ 15 ○ 16

Deep phosphate mines make up 80% of this tiny Pacific island.

Phosphate mining in Nauru

Apatite

This is the most common form of the pure element.

Red phosphorus

White phosphorus

This element remains stable in water, but catches fire on contact with air.

Chunk of violet phosphorus

Human skull

All bones, including those in the skull, are hardened by calcium phosphate.

Tuna

This fish is rich in phosphorus.

This purple color of the crystals is due to metal impurities.

This form of phosphorus is made in a laboratory by heating red phosphorus.

Phosphorus was accidently discovered by German alchemist Hennig Brand. In 1669, in his quest for the mythical Philosopher's Stone (a material some believed could turn any metal into gold), he boiled a large pot full of urine for days. This produced a mysterious glowing substance, which he called phosphorus, meaning "giver of light." Phosphorus is the first element to have a discoverer with a recorded name. It is never pure in nature, and occurs in different minerals. Phosphorus has several flammable,

Uses

This light, strong china contains calcium phosphate.

China tea set

Spraying ammonium phosphate over burning material cuts off its supply of oxygen. This extinguishes the fire.

Fire extinguisher

LIFE'S BUILDING BLOCKS

DNA—short for deoxyribonucleic acid—is like a mini database packed with instructions telling your body how to work properly. It consists of a chain of molecules and looks like a twisted ladder called a double helix. The edges are sugar molecules linked together by units containing phosphorus.

Sugar

Phosphate unit

These flexible fibers are composed of phosphate-rich glass.

Fiberoptics

Safety match box

The striking surface on the sides of the box contains phosphorus, which ignites the match upon contact.

Spraying crops with phosphates kills pests, such as insects.

Pesticides

Fertilizer

This fertilizer contains ammonium phosphate to boost plant growth.

solid forms, including **red**, **white**, black, and **violet**. The glow seen by Brand was caused by white phosphorus reacting with oxygen. Phosphorus is mainly found in **phosphate** minerals (in which phosphorus links to oxygen), such as **apatite**, its main ore.

Phosphates are present in **fine china**, and are an important ingredient in **fertilizers**. The strips on the sides of **safety match boxes** contain pure phosphorus. More complex phosphorus compounds used in **pesticides** are poisonous.

33 As Arsenic

State: **Solid**
⊖ 33　⊕ 33　◯ 42　Discovery: c. 1250

Forms

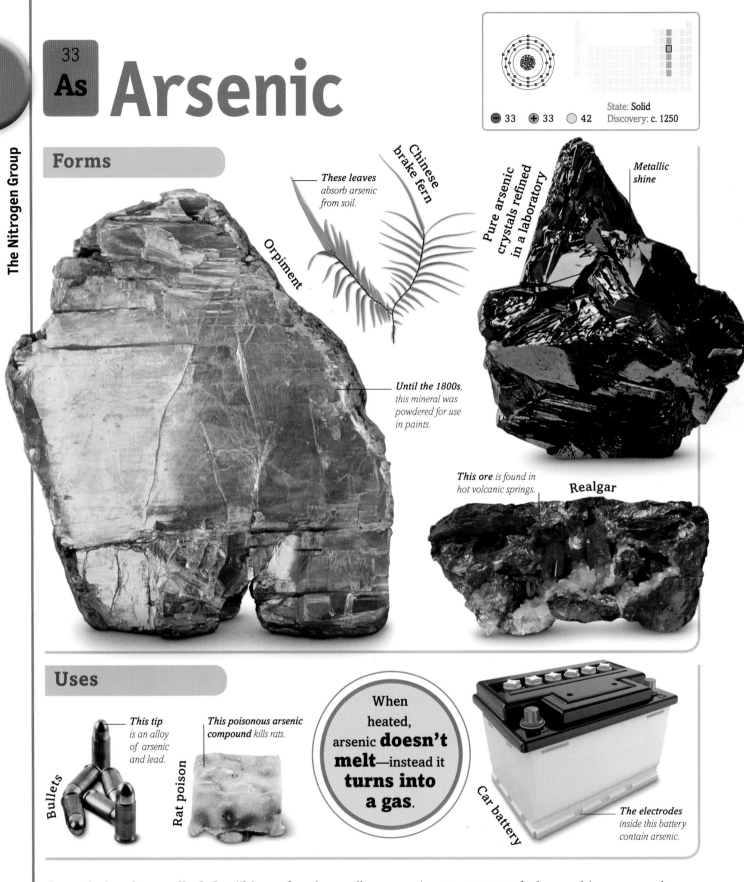

Chinese brake fern

These leaves absorb arsenic from soil.

Orpiment

Pure arsenic crystals refined in a laboratory

Metallic shine

Until the 1800s, this mineral was powdered for use in paints.

This ore is found in hot volcanic springs.

Realgar

Uses

This tip is an alloy of arsenic and lead.

Bullets

This poisonous arsenic compound kills rats.

Rat poison

When heated, arsenic **doesn't melt**—instead it **turns into a gas**.

Car battery

The electrodes inside this battery contain arsenic.

Arsenic is often called the "king of poisons." Every form of arsenic—either pure or in a compound—is poisonous to animals. In fact, arsenic poisons have been used for centuries. This semimetal is found in several minerals with striking colors, including **orpiment**. Naturally occurring **pure arsenic** has a shiny, gray color. Arsenic compounds are used in making some **rat poisons**. The leading use of arsenic today is for strengthening lead. This is done by mixing arsenic with lead to create a tough alloy that is often used in **car batteries**.

51
Sb Antimony

State: **Solid**
● 51 ⊕ 51 ○ 71 Discovery: c. 1600 BCE

Forms

Jamesonite

These needlelike crystals contain antimony, lead, and iron.

This mineral tarnishes on contact with air.

Stibnite

This silvery semimetal is hard but brittle.

Pure antimony crystals refined in a laboratory

Uses

These metallic letters are used by some printing presses, and are made of an antimony-tin -lead alloy.

Printing press metal type

These matches with antimony in the tip burn brighter than the ones without it.

Safety matches

Kohl is a dark eyeshadow.

Egyptian kohl

Kohl makes it **easier to see** in strong sunlight.

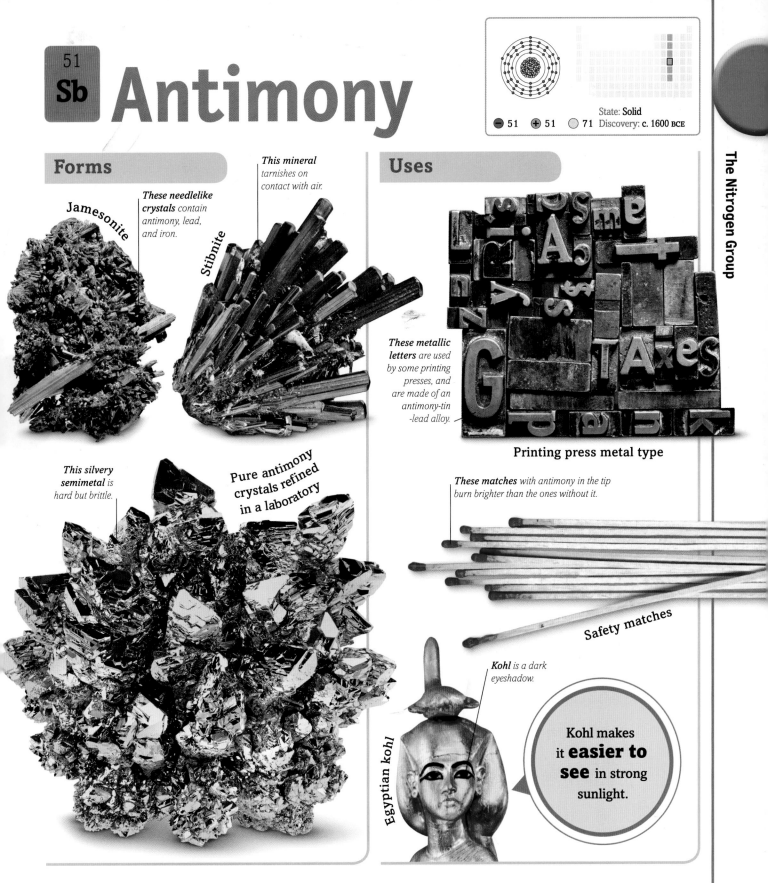

Antimony gets its name from the Greek word *anti-monos*, meaning "not alone." This may refer to the fact that the element is never found pure in nature, but is always found combined with heavier metals, such as lead. The element's symbol, Sb, comes from *stibium*, the Latin word for kohl, a form of eye makeup. The mineral ore **stibnite** is the largest source of **pure antimony**. Its pure form is mostly used to make hard alloys, such as that in the **metal type** used by some printers. Ancient **Egyptian kohl** was made from powdered stibnite.

161

83
Bi Bismuth

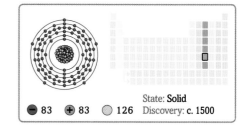

State: **Solid**
— 83   + 83   ○ 126   Discovery: **c. 1500**

Forms

This mineral is the main source of pure bismuth.

Bismuthinite

> In Earth's crust, bismuth is about **twice as abundant as gold**.

These rainbow colors form when the metal on the surface begins to react with oxygen.

Hopper crystals refined in a laboratory

These bismuth crystals were produced in a laboratory.

Bismuth is a radioactive element but its atoms are relatively stable and last for millions of years. People have known about bismuth for centuries. The Incas of South America added it to weapons made of the alloy bronze to harden them, while ancient Egyptians used a bismuth mineral to make their cosmetics glittery. Pure bismuth forms an oxide in air that is seen as colorful crystals called **hopper crystals**. This element is very brittle and has few uses when not in a compound form. Yellow bismuth

Uses

This cold box uses a compound called bismuth telluride, which becomes cold when electrified, and keeps items cool.

Portable refrigerator

This nail polish gives a pearly effect because of bismuth compounds.

Yellow cosmetics

This medicine contains a bismuth compound that helps settle an upset stomach.

Digestive medicine

Unlike most elements, bismuth's liquid state is **heavier** than its solid.

pigments are used in paints and **cosmetics**, while several bismuth compounds are also in **medicines**. An alloy of bismuth and tin is an ingredient in fire sprinklers.

115
Mc Moscovium

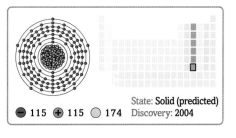

State: **Solid (predicted)**
⊖ 115   ⊕ 115   ◯ 174   Discovery: 2004

This is one of the machines in this research center.

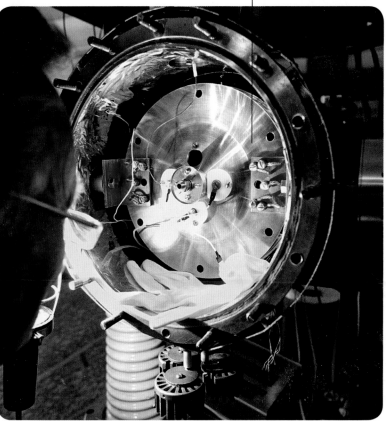

Joint Institute for Nuclear Research, Dubna, Russia

Only about a hundred or so atoms of this heavy, artificial element have been made. Moscovium was first created at the **Joint Institute for Nuclear Research** in Dubna, Russia. A team of Russian scientists, led by Yuri Oganessian, created this element by smashing americium atoms with parts of calcium atoms. It is named after the Russian capital city of Moscow. This element is extremely radioactive, and its atoms break up within a fraction of a second. Scientists think that moscovium would be a dense, metallic solid but with such small samples, they can only measure how big the atoms are before they break up.

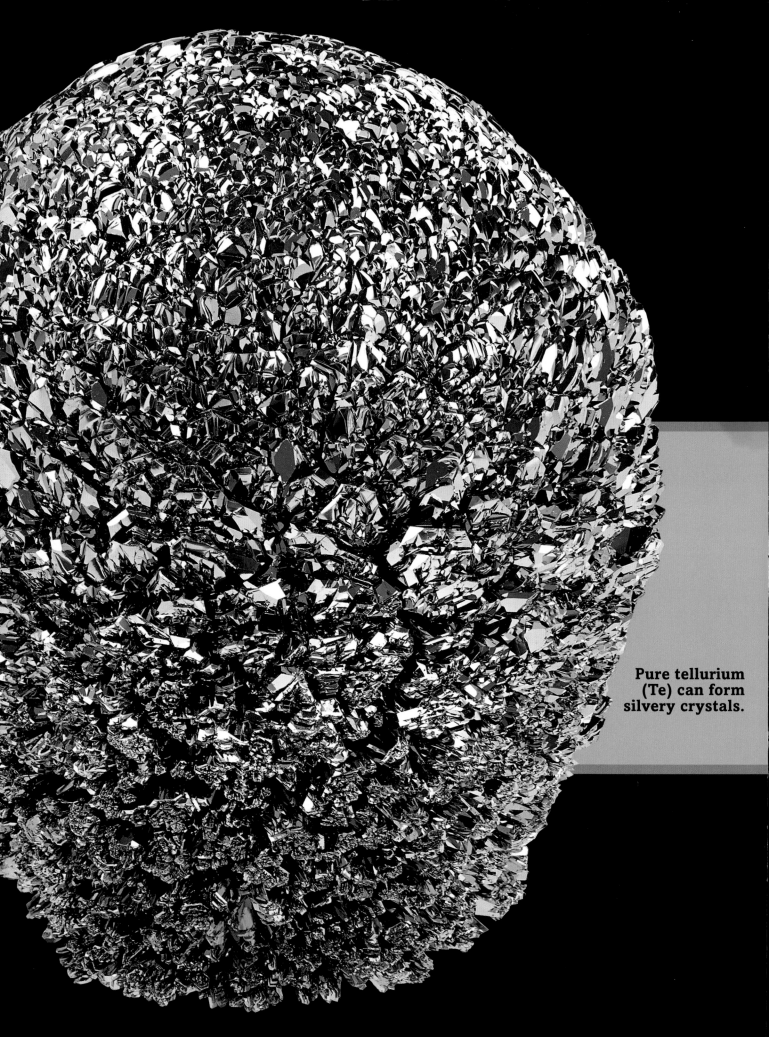

Pure tellurium
(Te) can form
silvery crystals.

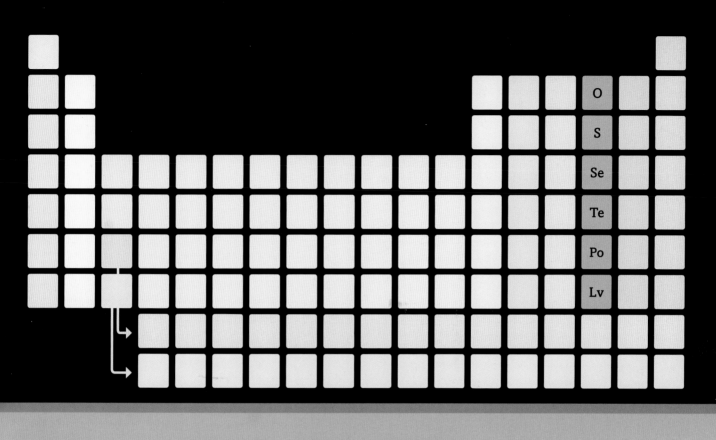

The Oxygen Group

This group does not include any natural metals. The first two members, oxygen (O) and sulfur (S), are nonmetals widespread in nature. The remaining three natural elements are semimetals. Only the artificial member, livermorium (Lv), is thought to be a metal, but chemists don't really know for sure.

Atomic structure
All members have six electrons in the outer shell of each atom. This electron structure makes these elements highly reactive.

Physical properties
The members of this group are solids, except oxygen (O), which is a gas at room temperature. The density of the elements increases down the group.

Chemical properties
The reactivity of these elements decreases down the group. Oxygen is always involved in the process of combustion.

Compounds
These elements can form compounds with each other. They all react with carbon (C) to form compounds, some with strong smells.

8 O Oxygen

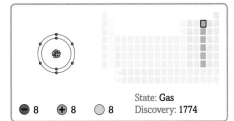

8 ⊕ 8 ○ 8
State: **Gas**
Discovery: 1774

Forms

Pure oxygen in a glass sphere

This glass sphere *traps pure oxygen, which produces a silver-blue glow when electrified.*

Streaks of light *adorn the sky as atoms of oxygen in the air are hit by a stream of particles blasting from the Sun.*

Northern lights

Plants *release oxygen in sunlight.*

Flames *are produced when oxygen reacts with fuel, such as wood.*

Fire

Sunflowers

Each water molecule *has two atoms of hydrogen and one of oxygen.*

Water

WHAT IS COMBUSTION?

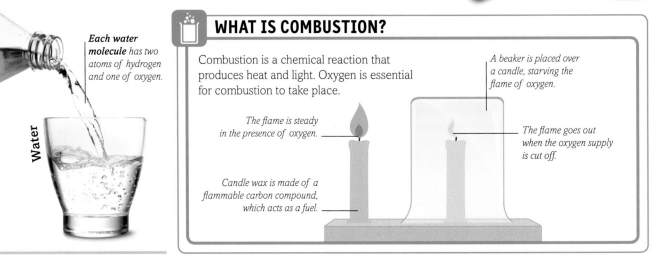

Combustion is a chemical reaction that produces heat and light. Oxygen is essential for combustion to take place.

The flame is steady in the presence of oxygen.

Candle wax is made of a flammable carbon compound, which acts as a fuel.

A beaker is placed over a candle, starving the flame of oxygen.

The flame goes out when the oxygen supply is cut off.

Oxygen is the most common element in Earth's crust. Oxygen and its compounds make up half of all rocks and minerals on our planet. In the atmosphere, **pure oxygen** makes up around one-fifth of the air. This element is a transparent gas. Life on Earth depends on oxygen for survival. Animals inhale air to collect the oxygen in it. Our bodies' cells then use that oxygen to break apart sugars to release energy, which powers our bodies. Another process that involves oxygen is the burning reaction called combustion, in which oxygen reacts with a fuel

Uses

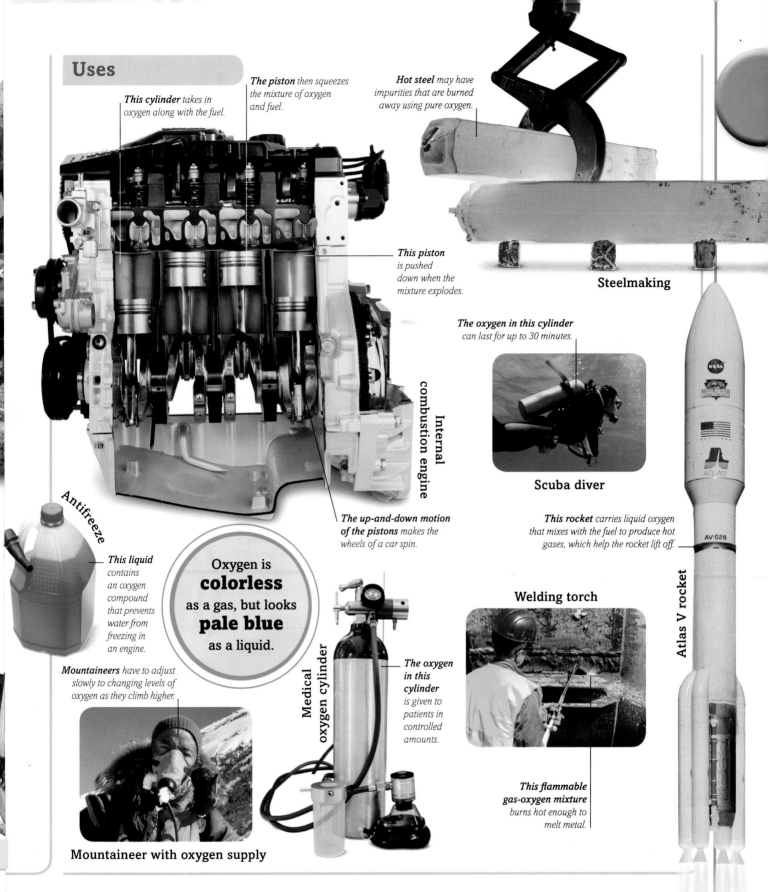

This cylinder takes in oxygen along with the fuel.

The piston then squeezes the mixture of oxygen and fuel.

Hot steel may have impurities that are burned away using pure oxygen.

Steelmaking

This piston is pushed down when the mixture explodes.

Internal combustion engine

The oxygen in this cylinder can last for up to 30 minutes.

Scuba diver

The up-and-down motion of the pistons makes the wheels of a car spin.

This rocket carries liquid oxygen that mixes with the fuel to produce hot gases, which help the rocket lift off.

Atlas V rocket

AV-028

ATLAS

Antifreeze

This liquid contains an oxygen compound that prevents water from freezing in an engine.

Oxygen is **colorless** as a gas, but looks **pale blue** as a liquid.

Mountaineers have to adjust slowly to changing levels of oxygen as they climb higher.

Medical oxygen cylinder

The oxygen in this cylinder is given to patients in controlled amounts.

Welding torch

This flammable gas-oxygen mixture burns hot enough to melt metal.

Mountaineer with oxygen supply

and produces **fire**. Oxygen is also used up when it reacts with other elements to form compounds called oxides. However, it is replenished by **plants** through a process called photosynthesis, which releases fresh oxygen. Car **engines** are powered by the combustion of gasoline or other fuels. Oxygen is also useful in the **making of steel**. Tanks of oxygen let **mountaineers** breathe easily in environments that have low levels of this gas. Rockets, such as the **Atlas V**, carry liquid oxygen to burn fuel in the absence of air in space.

DANAKIL DEPRESSION

This hot spring in Africa's Danakil Depression is surrounded by a yellow crust of pure sulfur. The sunken region between Ethiopia and Eritrea in East Africa is a wild volcanic area, packed with erupting craters, arid deserts, boiling mud, and pools with unusual colors caused by the presence of sulfur and many mineral salts.

At more than 330 ft (100 m) below sea level, the Danakil Depression is one of the lowest points on Earth's surface. This area receives little or no rainfall and the weather is hot and dry, with temperatures soaring above 120°F (50°C). The scalding green water of the springs inside the depression contains pure sulfur as well as a toxic sulfur compound called sulfuric acid. As the water evaporates, sulfur deposits build up around the edges of the pools, making beautiful shapes across the vast landscape. Tourists visit to marvel at the remarkable sights at Danakil, even though the inhospitable conditions in the area give it the title of the "cruelest place on Earth."

34
Se Selenium

State: **Solid**
Discovery: 1817

⊖ 34 ⊕ 34 ◯ 45

Forms

This form of the element has a metallic sheen on its surface.

Chunk of pure gray selenium refined in a laboratory

Brazil nuts

These nuts are the richest food source of selenium.

These dark areas contain selenium and copper.

Berzelianite

Uses

This calculator is powered by a solar cell made of selenium and nickel.

Calculator

Anti-dandruff shampoo

A selenium compound in this shampoo treats dandruff.

This bright color comes from the red selenium in the glaze.

Ceramic vase

Photocopier

Many office photocopiers use selenium in powdered form.

Selenium is named after Selene, the Greek goddess of the Moon. This element is a semimetal and so has the properties of both metals and nonmetals. Selenium has two main pure forms: **gray selenium**, which is a hard substance, and red selenium, which is a soft powder. The most common use of selenium is as an ingredient that provides color in glass and **ceramics**. Selenium is sensitive to light, so it is used in solar cells that convert sunlight into electricity. It is also utilized in **photocopy machines**.

172

52
Te Tellurium

State: **Solid**
Discovery: 1783

⊖ 52   ⊕ 52   ○ 76

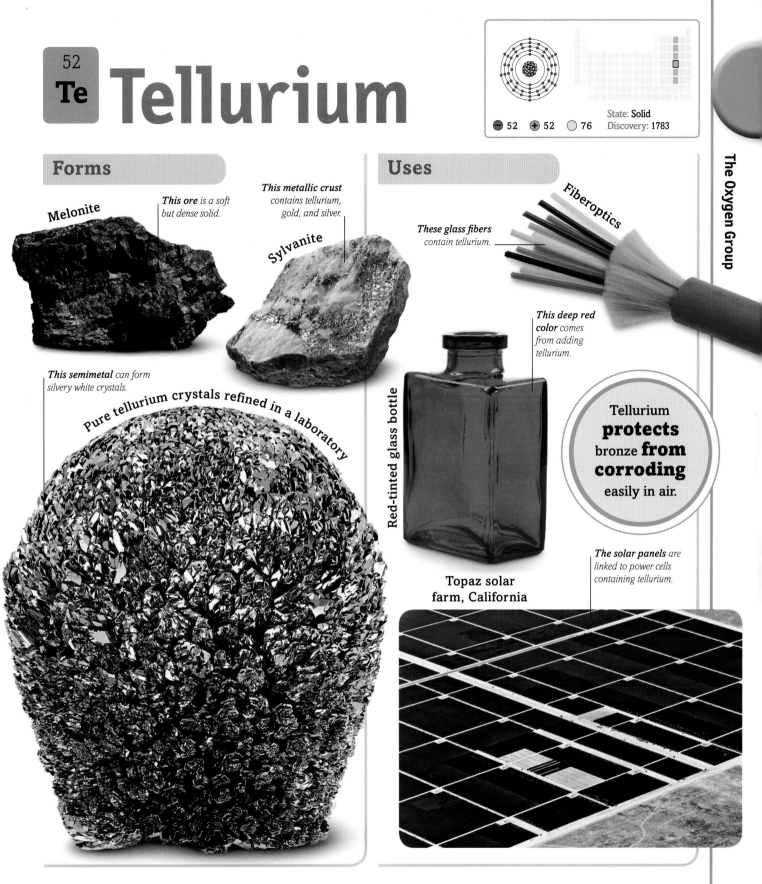

Forms

Melonite

This ore *is a soft but dense solid.*

This metallic crust *contains tellurium, gold, and silver.*

Sylvanite

This semimetal *can form silvery white crystals.*

Pure tellurium crystals refined in a laboratory

Uses

Fiberoptics

These glass fibers *contain tellurium.*

This deep red color *comes from adding tellurium.*

Red-tinted glass bottle

Tellurium **protects** bronze **from corroding** easily in air.

The solar panels *are linked to power cells containing tellurium.*

Topaz solar farm, California

Tellurium is one of the ten rarest elements on this planet. It gets its name from the Latin word *tellus*, which means Earth. This element is often found as a compound with another element, such as the metal nickel, as in the case of the ore **melonite**. Tellurium is also produced as a waste product when lead and copper are refined. **Pure tellurium** can take on two forms: a shiny, metallic solid or a brown powder. This element is mainly used in the glass of **fiberoptics**—fibers that carry high volumes of information much faster than copper cables.

173

84
Po Polonium

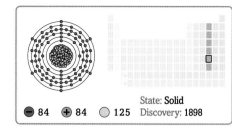

State: Solid
Discovery: 1898

− 84 + 84 ○ 125

Forms

This uranium ore contains **0.0000001 percent** polonium.

Uraninite

This mineral contains uranium atoms that break apart to form atoms of polonium.

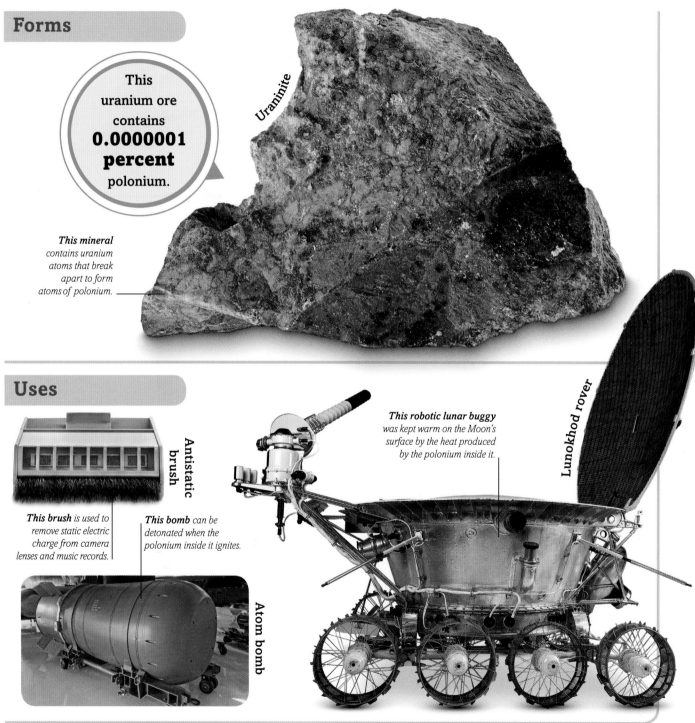

Uses

Antistatic brush

This brush is used to remove static electric charge from camera lenses and music records.

This bomb can be detonated when the polonium inside it ignites.

Atom bomb

This robotic lunar buggy was kept warm on the Moon's surface by the heat produced by the polonium inside it.

Lunokhod rover

Polonium is very radioactive: 0.03 oz (1 g) of this metal quickly heats up to 932°F (500°C) because of the radiation it emits. This element was discovered by Marie and Pierre Curie in 1898. Marie named it after Poland, her homeland. It is rare in nature, and is normally produced in nuclear reactors. Despite its radioactivity, this element is used in a few ways. It can trigger the explosion of **atom bombs**. It heats and powers spacecraft, such as the Russian **Lunokhod rovers**, which landed on the Moon in the 1970s.

116 Lv Livermorium

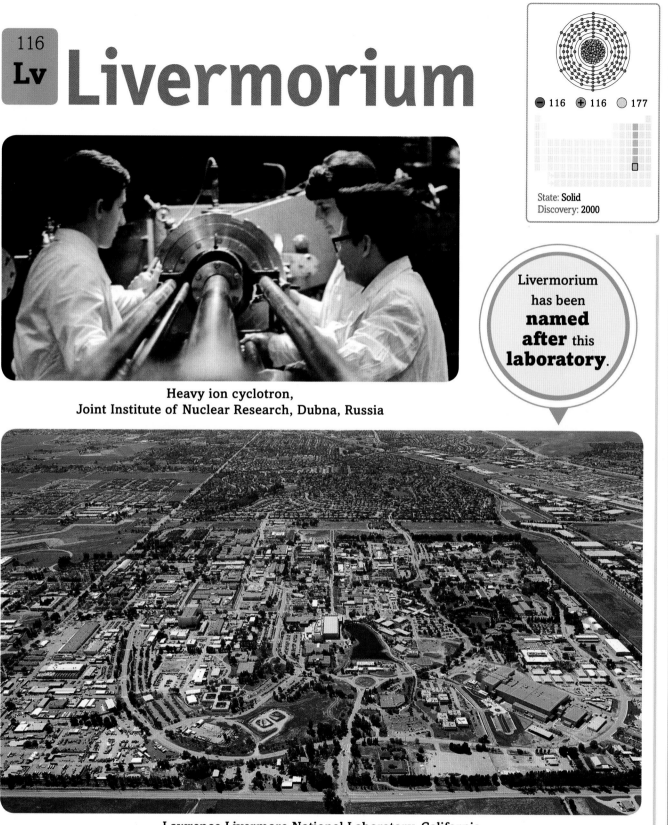

- 116 + 116 ○ 177

State: **Solid**
Discovery: **2000**

Heavy ion cyclotron,
Joint Institute of Nuclear Research, Dubna, Russia

Livermorium
has been
**named
after** this
laboratory.

Lawrence Livermore National Laboratory, California

When livermorium atoms were first produced in 2000, they broke apart in a fraction of a second. The first successful attempt to create atoms of this element was made at the **Joint Institute of Nuclear Research** at Dubna, Russia. The team worked with material provided by the **Lawrence Livermore National Laboratory** in California. This highly radioactive element was produced by firing calcium atoms at curium atoms in a particle accelerator (a machine in which atoms are smashed together).

This glass sphere contains pure iodine (I).

																	F
																	Cl
																	Br
																	I
																	At
																	Ts

The Halogen Group

One of the most reactive groups in the periodic table, this set includes nonmetals. The name "halogen" means "salt former," which refers to the way elements in this group react with metals to form salts, such as sodium chloride, widely known as common salt. Scientists don't know much about tennessine (Ts), an artificial halogen.

Atomic structure
All members have seven electrons in the outer shell of each atom. There is space for one more electron in each outer shell.

Physical properties
Bromine (Br) is the only liquid halogen. Fluorine (F) and chlorine (Cl) are gases, while iodine and astatine (At) are solids.

Chemical properties
Every halogen atom receives one electron from other atoms to form a compound. Reactivity decreases down the group.

Compounds
The halogens react with hydrogen (H) to form acidic compounds. Halogen compounds are used in products such as bleach.

9 F Fluorine

State: **Gas**
Discovery: 1886
− 9 + 9 ○ 10

State: **Gas**

Laboratory sample

Forms

This soft mineral is brittle, which means it breaks easily into lots of pieces.

Cryolite

This sealed case contains a mixture of fluorine and helium.

Topaz **means "fire"** in the ancient Indian language of Sanskrit.

These cubic crystals are green due to impurities.

Topaz

Fluorite

This precious gemstone contains 20.7% fluorine.

This highly reactive element is incredibly dangerous when pure: just a tiny amount added to the air can kill a person. A pale yellow gas, fluorine reacts with brick, glass, and steel, burning a hole straight through them. Because it is so dangerous, pure fluorine is often stored in nickel containers that can resist its attack. Minerals such as **cryolite** and **fluorite** contain this element. This gas and its less harmful compounds have a wide variety of uses. Hydrofluoric acid is a toxic liquid used to etch patterns on glass, as seen in some **glass vases**.

Uses

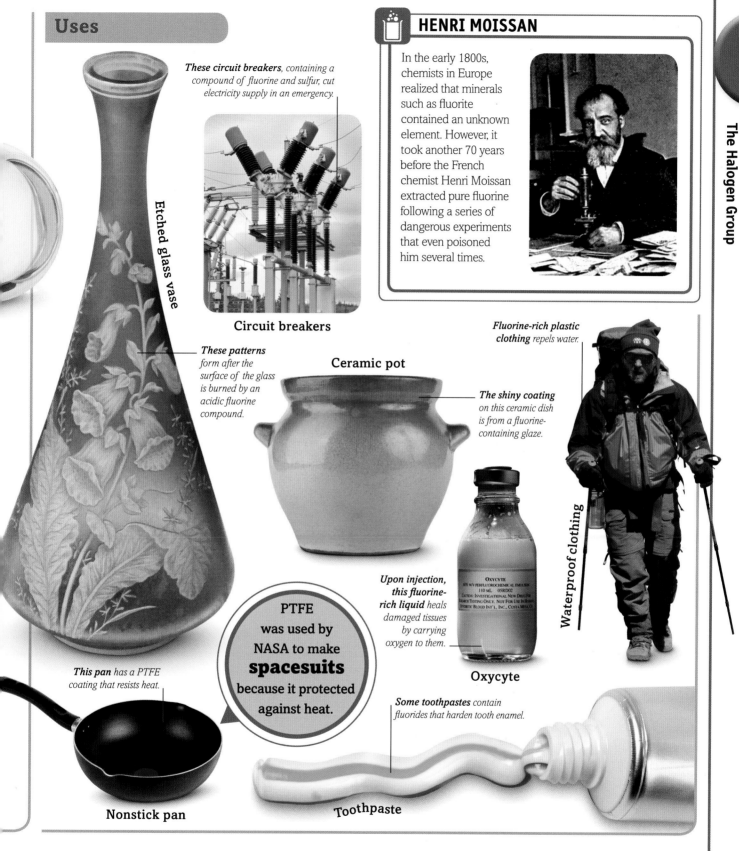

These circuit breakers, containing a compound of fluorine and sulfur, cut electricity supply in an emergency.

Circuit breakers

Etched glass vase

These patterns form after the surface of the glass is burned by an acidic fluorine compound.

Ceramic pot

The shiny coating on this ceramic dish is from a fluorine-containing glaze.

Fluorine-rich plastic clothing repels water.

Waterproof clothing

HENRI MOISSAN

In the early 1800s, chemists in Europe realized that minerals such as fluorite contained an unknown element. However, it took another 70 years before the French chemist Henri Moissan extracted pure fluorine following a series of dangerous experiments that even poisoned him several times.

The Halogen Group

PTFE was used by NASA to make **spacesuits** because it protected against heat.

Upon injection, this fluorine-rich liquid heals damaged tissues by carrying oxygen to them.

Oxycyte

This pan has a PTFE coating that resists heat.

Nonstick pan

Some toothpastes contain fluorides that harden tooth enamel.

Toothpaste

Some glazes used to coat ceramics contain fluorine minerals. When heated, these glazes release fluorine, which hardens the ceramic underneath. Another compound called polytetrafluoroethylene (PTFE) is commonly used to make **nonstick pans**: this material is slippery and prevents food that has burned while cooking from sticking to the pan. Thin fibers made of PTFE are also used to make lightweight, **waterproof clothing**. One of the most common uses of fluorine compounds is in **toothpaste**: they toughen teeth against decay.

Cl 17 Chlorine

State: **Gas**
Discovery: 1774

- 17 + 17 ○ 18

Forms

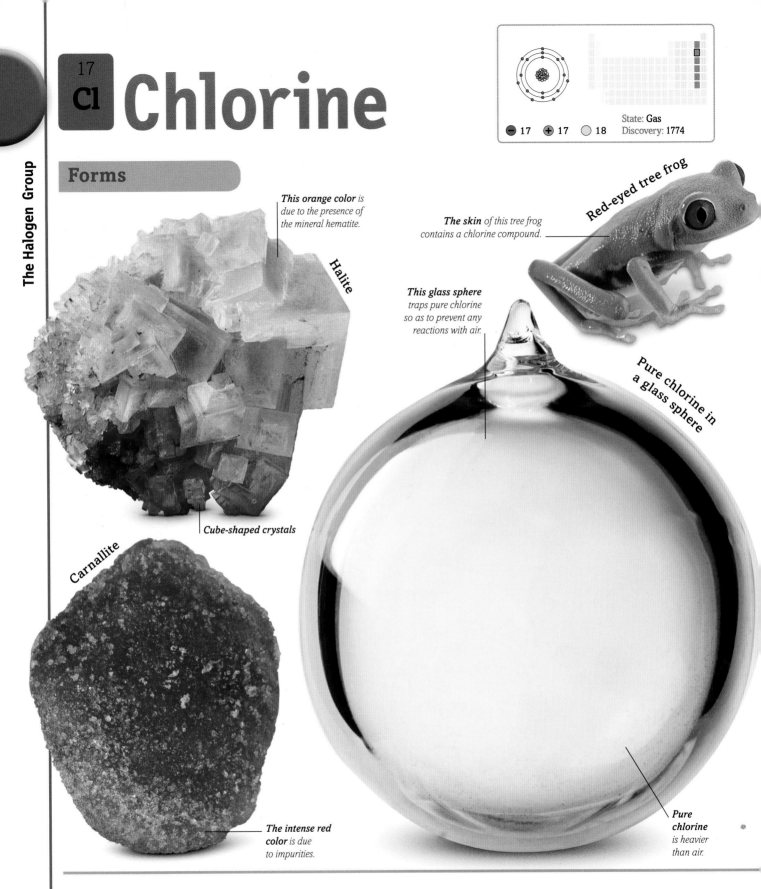

This orange color is due to the presence of the mineral hematite.

Halite

Cube-shaped crystals

Carnallite

The intense red color is due to impurities.

The skin of this tree frog contains a chlorine compound.

Red-eyed tree frog

This glass sphere traps pure chlorine so as to prevent any reactions with air.

Pure chlorine in a glass sphere

Pure chlorine is heavier than air.

Chlorine is named after the Greek word *chlóros* which means "pale green," a reference to the color of this gaseous element. Chlorine is a highly reactive gas that forms a number of compounds, and does not exist pure in nature. The most common chlorine compound is sodium chloride, found in nature as the mineral **halite**. Chlorine compounds are important for the body and are used by muscles and nerves. They are also present in sweat. Because it is poisonous in its pure form, chlorine gas was used as a weapon during World War I: soldiers had to wear masks for

Running shoes

The soles of some **running shoes** *contain chlorine compounds.*

Sodium chloride *is used to season meals.*

Common salt

Chloroform

Breathing in *this chlorine-infused liquid makes people fall unconscious.*

The chlorine levels in this pool *need to be regulated carefully to maintain the quality of water.*

Swimming pool

CHLORINATION

The process of cleaning dirty water with chlorine is called chlorination. This method involves passing the water through a filter.

1. Dirty water enters the tank.

2. The filter traps tiny particles of impurities.

3. Chlorine mixed in water kills the remaining germs.

4. Clean water for drinking, cooking, and washing is released.

PVC pipes

Strong water **pipes** *are composed of thick PVC.*

This chlorine-rich **plastic** *is tough.*

Safety goggles

Bleach

This case *is tough but flexible.*

This bleach cleaner *contains a compound called sodium hypochlorite.*

PVC suitcase

protection against this weapon. Today, chlorine is used in many ways. Its compounds are present in everything from **running shoes** to **chloroform**. It reacts with hydrogen to make hydrochloric acid, an industrial cleaner. This corrosive liquid eats away at most metals, releasing hydrogen gas. A weaker

chlorine acid is used to clean water in **swimming pools**, while **bleach** and other cleaners use chlorine compounds to kill germs. One of the most widely used plastics, **polyvinyl chloride (PVC)**, contains chlorine. It is a tough plastic, used to make many rigid objects.

OCEAN CLEAN UP
Chlorine is common in cleaning products, and can be used for scrubbing everything from bathroom tiles to ocean floors. These divers are trying to remove harmful seaweed in the Mediterranean Sea using the power of chlorine. The green weed grows quickly and can potentially kill other sea plants by depriving them of their essential nutrients. Some fish are also poisoned if they eat this toxic weed.

The two divers use chlorine twice in the cleaning process. First, they cover the thick seaweed with a sheet made of PVC, a tough plastic containing chlorine. Next, they pump a compound of sodium and chlorine called sodium hypochlorite under the sheet. This powerful liquid bleach kills the unwanted seaweed. Several weeks later, the divers return to remove the PVC sheets. The invading seaweed will not regrow, and the plants on the seabed will gradually return. Although chlorine is highly reactive and can damage skin and other body parts, divers are well protected by their rubber wetsuits.

35 Br Bromine

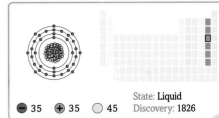

State: **Liquid**
Discovery: 1826

⊖ 35   ⊕ 35   ◯ 45

Forms

Bromine vapor

Pure bromine in a glass sphere

This sealed glass container prevents bromine vapor from escaping.

Potassium bromide

Pure bromine is a red-brown liquid.

Bromine
is named after
the Greek word for
"stench"
because of its
strong smell.

Bromine is the only nonmetal that is a liquid at room temperature. A thick vapor given off by this liquid is dangerous if inhaled. **Pure bromine** is never found in nature. Its compounds can easily mix in water, and are found dissolved in seawater and extremely salty lakes, such as the **Dead Sea** in the Middle East. Solid bromine salts, including **potassium bromide**, collect as the water evaporates, leaving behind crusts of white crystals. Bromine can then be extracted from the solid salts. A common

Uses

This bromine salt was used in the late 19th century to help patients sleep.

Bromine chemical test kit

Cl	Br	pH
5	10	8.2
3	6	7.8
2	4	7.5
1	2	7.2
.5	1	6.8

MAX — MAX
MIN — MIN

The colors on this test kit *show how much bromine is in the water.*

Bromine
was used as a
weapon
in World War I.

Crusts of bromine salts form along the Israeli shoreline.

The Dead Sea Coast

Fire extinguisher

Chubb Fire
HALON

This fire extinguisher uses a nonflammable, bromine-rich gas to extinguish fires.

This image was created when light reacted with silver bromide.

Photograph negative

The fabric used to make this suit contains bromine compounds that make it fireproof.

Fireproof suit

👓 ANTOINE-JÉRÔME BALARD

In 1826, French chemist Antoine-Jérôme Balard discovered bromine. He heated seawater from salt marshes, and after most of the water had evaporated, he passed chlorine gas through what was left. The remaining liquid turned orange-red: this was bromine.

use of this element is as a disinfectant to clean water. It works better than chlorine in hot tubs because chlorine escapes into the air easily from the warm water. The concentration of bromine in swimming pools can be regulated using **chemical test kits**. Bromine compounds can be used in film photography in which images are printed using chemicals on **negatives**. Today, bromine is mainly used in **fireproof material**, such as firefighter suits or furnishings, because it doesn't catch fire easily.

53
I Iodine

State: **Solid**
⊖ 53 ⊕ 53 ○ 74   Discovery: 1811

Forms

Pure iodine in a glass sphere

This sealed glass container prevents iodine from reacting with air.

Purple iodine vapour

Purple-black solid iodine

Solid iodine **does not melt** when heated, but turns into a vapor.

Crab

This crab absorbs iodine from seawater.

Uses

Printing ink

These colored inks are made using iodine compounds.

Polarizing sunglasses

These lenses contain iodine, which filters out bright, reflected light.

Candied cherries

The bright red color of these cherries is due to an iodine dye.

This disinfectant is applied to wounds to stop the spread of infection.

Betadine

Betadine dermique 10%
Solution pour application locale
MEDA Pharma 08920.3   10 ml

Iodine is the only halogen that is solid at room temperature. The element forms a purple gas when heated, and is named after the Greek word *iodes*, which means "violet." Iodine was first discovered in seaweed, and many plants and animals in the sea have high levels of iodine.

Seafood, including **crabs** and fish, provide the element in our diet. The human body needs small amounts of iodine to make an important substance called thyroxine, which helps us grow. Iodine is also used to make **printing ink**, red and brown food dyes, and disinfectants.

186

85 At Astatine

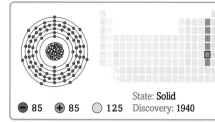

State: **Solid** Discovery: **1940**
● 85 ⊕ 85 ○ 125

Atoms of astatine are unstable, and typically break down after just a few hours, into atoms of lighter elements, such as bismuth. This radioactive element itself forms in a similar way when atoms of a heavier element called francium break apart. Tiny amounts of this rare element are found in uranium ores, such as **uraninite**. The Italian physicist Emilio Segrè was one of the first scientists to isolate a sample of pure astatine. He was able to do so by using a particle accelerator: this is a machine that smashes together atoms and then studies the results.

Inside this mineral, unstable atoms of the element francium are breaking apart, forming astatine atoms.

Uraninite

117 Ts Tennessine

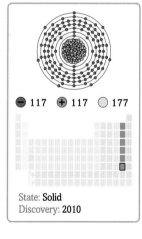

State: **Solid** Discovery: **2010**
● 117 ⊕ 117 ○ 177

Nuclear Reactor, Oak Ridge National Laboratory, Tennessee

Atoms of tennessine **existed for a few seconds** after they were formed.

Tennessine is the youngest element in the periodic table. It was produced in 2010, in the Russian city of Dubna. The element was named after the state of Tennessee, home to the **Oak Ridge National Laboratory**, which houses one of the first large-scale nuclear reactors ever built. Only a few atoms of this halogen element have ever been made. Even so, scientists think that it is a semimetal, not a nonmetal like all the other halogens.

Krypton (Kr)
becomes
visible only
when it is
electrified.

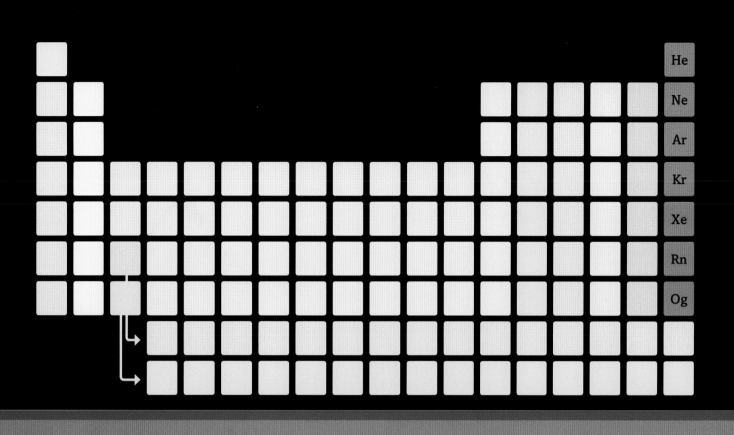

Noble Gases

The group on the far right of the periodic table belongs to the noble gases. These elements are described as "noble" because they do not react with the other "common" elements, such as oxygen (O). Their atoms never form bonds in nature, not even with atoms of their own kind, and so they are always gases at room temperature.

Atomic structure
Apart from a helium (He) atom that has two electrons in its outer shell, all other elements in this group have atoms with eight electrons.

Physical properties
All the members of this group are colorless gases. Going down the group, the density increases—radon (Rn) is 54 times denser than helium.

Chemical properties
Noble gases never react in nature. In the laboratory, heavier noble gases can be forced to form compounds with fluorine (F).

Compounds
These gases form no natural compounds. However, xenon (Xe), krypton (Kr), and argon (Ar) can be made to form compounds.

2 He Helium

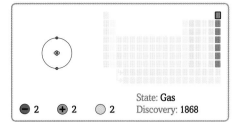

State: **Gas**
Discovery: **1868**

⊖ 2 ⊕ 2 ◯ 2

Forms

This sample of helium is trapped in a glass sphere.

Pure helium in a glass sphere

Helium is a transparent gas, but it glows purple when electrified.

Saturn

Saturn's atmosphere is made up of clouds of hydrogen and helium.

Natural gas often contains some helium.

Gas flare rig

Uses

A particle accelerator is a machine that smashes together atoms: this one uses liquid helium to cool its parts.

Large Hadron Collider, CERN, Switzerland

Helium-cooled MRI scanner

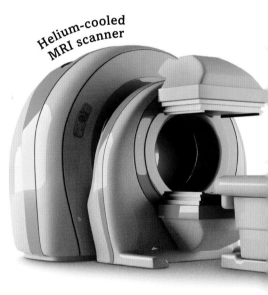

Helium is the second lightest element after hydrogen. This transparent gas was first discovered in 1868 by Sir William Ramsay, a Scottish chemist. Today, we know that a quarter of all the atoms in the universe are helium. It is one of the main gases in the atmospheres of giant gas planets, such as **Saturn**. Being so light, however, helium is very rare on Earth: it escapes from our atmosphere into space. It was not until 1895 that chemists managed to collect a sample of helium gas coming from uraninite, a radioactive uranium mineral. Today, helium is

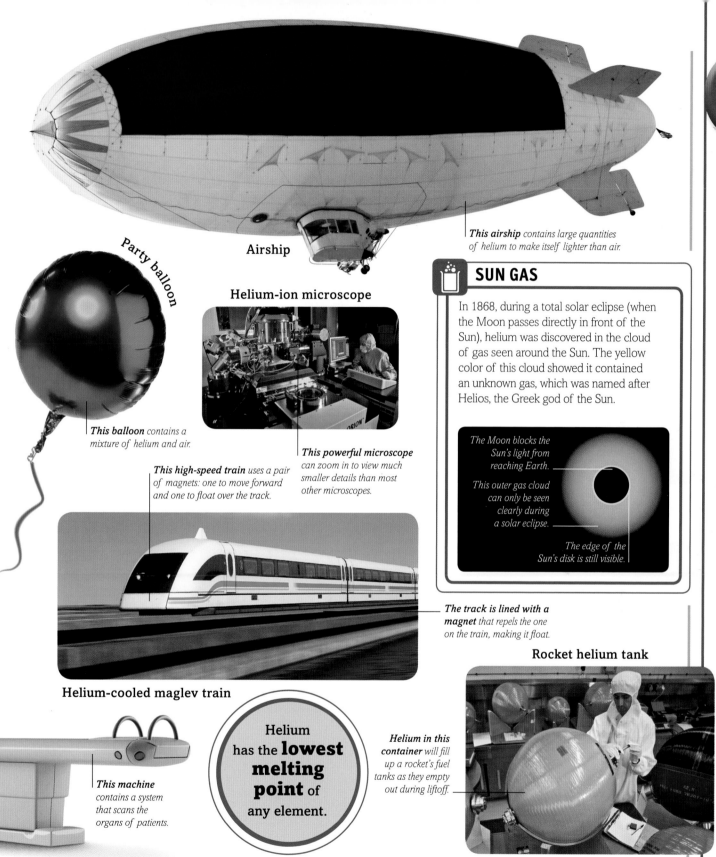

Party balloon

Airship

This airship contains large quantities of helium to make itself lighter than air.

Helium-ion microscope

This balloon contains a mixture of helium and air.

This powerful microscope can zoom in to view much smaller details than most other microscopes.

This high-speed train uses a pair of magnets: one to move forward and one to float over the track.

SUN GAS

In 1868, during a total solar eclipse (when the Moon passes directly in front of the Sun), helium was discovered in the cloud of gas seen around the Sun. The yellow color of this cloud showed it contained an unknown gas, which was named after Helios, the Greek god of the Sun.

The Moon blocks the Sun's light from reaching Earth.

This outer gas cloud can only be seen clearly during a solar eclipse.

The edge of the Sun's disk is still visible.

The track is lined with a magnet that repels the one on the train, making it float.

Rocket helium tank

Helium-cooled maglev train

This machine contains a system that scans the organs of patients.

Helium has the **lowest melting point** of any element.

Helium in this container will fill up a rocket's fuel tanks as they empty out during liftoff.

collected from underground reservoirs or is found mixed in natural **gas** and oil. Unlike hydrogen, which is very reactive, helium is a noble gas and does not react at all. This property makes it safe to use in objects such as **party balloons** and **airships**. To turn helium into a liquid, it must be cooled to an extreme temperature of −452°F (−269°C). Liquid helium is used to make things very cold, including the powerful magnets used to make **maglev trains** float along special tracks. **MRI scanners** also use liquid helium for cooling.

NEBULA
This glowing nebula (cloud of gas and dust) is the Crescent Nebula. It is so vast that our entire Solar System would fit inside it seven times over. The nebula's light comes from a super-heated star at its center. Known as WR 136, this star is 15 times heavier than our Sun and 250,000 times brighter. Its immense power comes from its fuel—helium.

Helium makes WR 136 hot and bright. The star once burned using hydrogen, like our Sun. Hydrogen atoms smashed together in the star's core until they became helium atoms, releasing energy in the process. However, the star ran out of hydrogen about 200,000 years ago. It began smashing together helium atoms instead, and ballooned into a gigantic red star, sending out a cloud of gas that spread around it. The star is producing a wind of electrified gases that hurtles out at 1,056 miles (1,700 km) every second. This wind continues to crash into the gas cloud, making it glow into the nebula we see. Eventually, WR 136 will run out of helium and its other fuels, and explode in an enormous fireball called a supernova.

10
Ne Neon

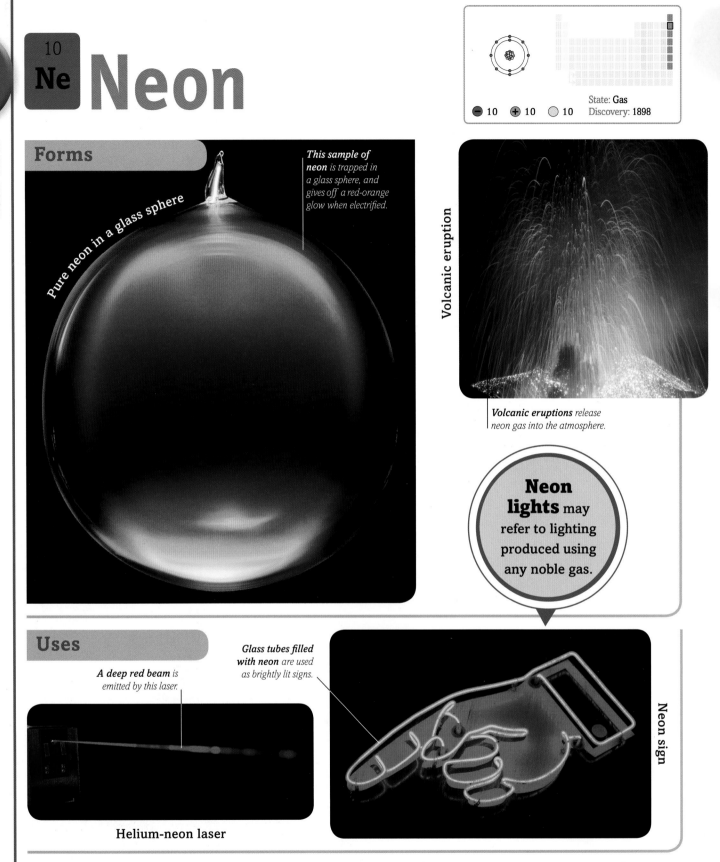

Forms

Pure neon in a glass sphere

This sample of neon *is trapped in a glass sphere, and gives off a red-orange glow when electrified.*

Volcanic eruption

Volcanic eruptions *release neon gas into the atmosphere.*

Neon lights may refer to lighting produced using any noble gas.

Uses

A deep red beam *is emitted by this laser.*

Glass tubes filled with neon *are used as brightly lit signs.*

Helium-neon laser

Neon sign

Neon is a rare element: it makes up just 0.001 percent of our atmosphere. Some of it was locked in Earth's rocks when the planet formed, and this is released into the air by **volcanic eruptions**. **Pure neon**, a transparent gas, is extracted by cooling air until it turns into a liquid and then allowing it to warm, causing each element to vaporize at a different temperature. Neon can be mixed with helium to create research **lasers**. However, it is most commonly used in lighting, such as in **illuminated signs** or as bright warning beacons in the path of aircraft at airports.

194

18
Ar Argon

State: **Gas**
Discovery: 1894

⊖ 18 ⊕ 18 ◯ 22

Forms

Pure argon in a glass sphere

This sample of argon is trapped in a glass sphere, and gives off a pale purple color when electrified.

The Magna Carta, *a historical document, is stored in argon, which forces out oxygen and water vapor that would damage the parchment.*

Argon-filled display

Uses

Argon-filled suit

Some diving suits *are inflated with argon to retain heat in cold water.*

Double-glazed window

The space between the glass panes *is filled with argon to slow the loss of heat.*

Metal welding

Argon in this flame *prevents metals from reacting with oxygen*

Argon is the third most abundant gas in the atmosphere, after nitrogen and oxygen. It undergoes no reactions with any other element, and was named after the Greek word *argos*, meaning "idle." Argon does not conduct heat well so it is put in **double-glazed windows**, and in **diving suits** during cold, deep dives. Its lack of reactivity is useful. Argon is used in **museum displays** to protect delicate exhibits. It also prevents metals reacting during hot **welding**. This element can also be useful in the production of titanium.

36 Kr Krypton

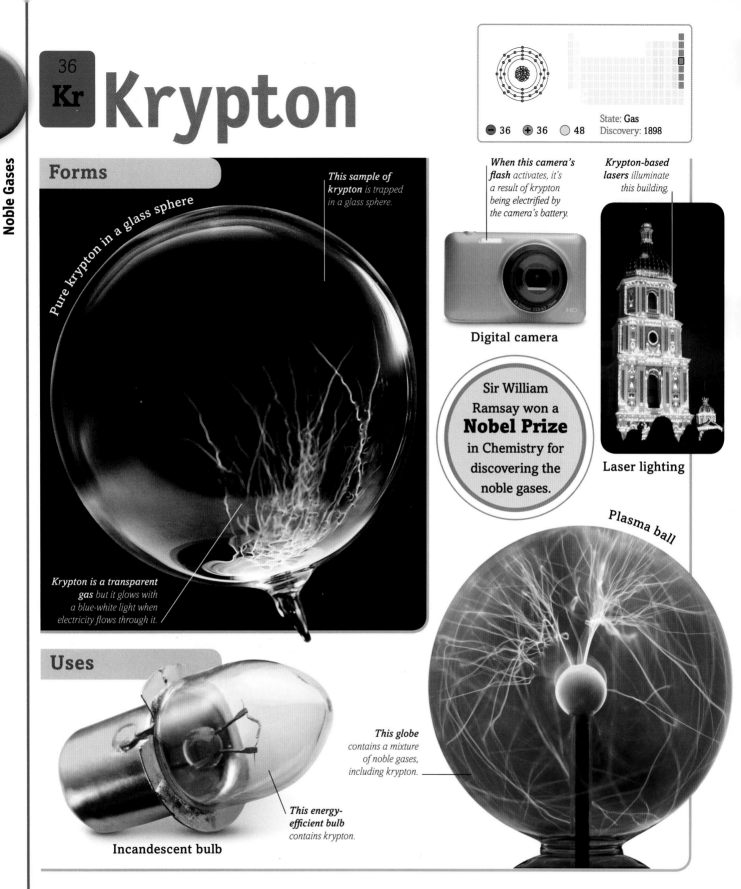

⊖ 36 ⊕ 36 ◯ 48 State: **Gas** Discovery: 1898

Forms

Pure krypton in a glass sphere

*This sample of **krypton** is trapped in a glass sphere.*

*Krypton is a transparent **gas** but it glows with a blue-white light when electricity flows through it.*

*When this camera's **flash** activates, it's a result of krypton being electrified by the camera's battery.*

Digital camera

*Krypton-based **lasers** illuminate this building.*

Laser lighting

Sir William Ramsay won a **Nobel Prize** in Chemistry for discovering the noble gases.

Plasma ball

Uses

This energy-efficient bulb contains krypton.

Incandescent bulb

This globe contains a mixture of noble gases, including krypton.

The word krypton means the "hidden one" in Greek. This element exists as an inert gas in nature, which means that it does not react with almost any other element. Krypton is not found in any minerals and only tiny amounts of it can be found in the air. **Pure krypton** produces a very bright white light when electrified with a current, which makes it ideal for use in **flash bulbs**. Krypton can react with the element fluorine to form the compound krypton fluoride, which is used to power some kinds of **laser**.

54 Xe Xenon

State: **Gas**
Discovery: **1898**

● 54 ⊕ 54 ○ 77

Forms

Pure xenon in a glass sphere

Xenon is a transparent gas but it glows with a blue light when an electric current flows through it.

This sample of xenon is trapped in a glass sphere.

Anesthesia machine

The xenon produced by this device makes a patient unconscious before an operation.

Xenon is used in powerful **lasers** that can **kill bacteria**.

Xenon glow disinfects the air in a room.

Xenon lamp

Car headlight

Xenon headlights glow brighter than the more common halogen headlights.

Uses

High pressure inside this lamp makes electrified xenon glow very brightly.

Modern film projector lamp

Electrified xenon blasts from the exhaust, pushing the probe forward.

Dawn space probe

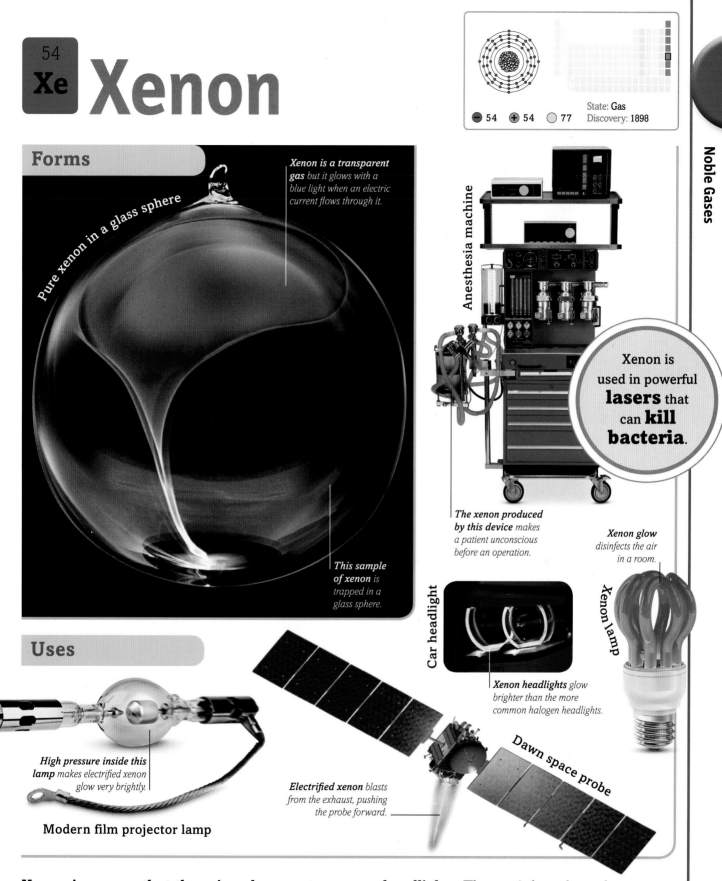

Xenon is so rare that there is only one atom of this gaseous element for every 10 million atoms in the air. Like the other noble gases, xenon is colorless and odorless. It glows brightly when electrified, making it useful in very powerful lamps, such as those used in **film projectors** and **car headlights**. The gas is harmless when breathed in and can be used as an **anesthetic**. When preparing food, **xenon lamps** can purify the air. To propel spacecraft, xenon is used in some rocket engines that produce streams of fast-moving, electrified atoms.

86 Rn Radon

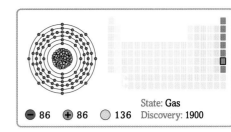

State: **Gas**
− 86   + 86   ○ 136   Discovery: 1900

This uranium mineral releases radon gas, as radioactive metals in it break apart.

These yellow crystals belong to another uranium mineral called uranophane.

Uraninite

It takes only 3.8 days for half of radon's atoms to split into atoms of other elements.

Glass sphere containing radon and air

Radon is the only natural radioactive noble gas. This element is produced by the breakdown of uranium and other radioactive metals. Being a gas, radon escapes from minerals, such as **uraninite**, into the air. Radon is very radioactive and inhaling it can cause illness, such as lung cancer. In most places, the amount of radon in the air is incredibly tiny. However, its levels are high around **volcanic springs** and mud, where it bubbles out with other hot gases. Radon is also present in the water at **geothermal power plants**, which use heat energy from deep, volcanic rocks to make electricity. Radon is more common in areas rich in granite rock. In these places, people use **test kits** to monitor the radon level in their homes.

As it decays, a compound called thorium dioxide emits radon.

The muddy water *from volcanic springs contains radon.*

Hot springs in Lisvori, Greece

These pipes *draw water containing radon from deep under the ground, and this is then used to power the plant.*

Geothermal power plant

This kit *collects radon from the air so the amount of the gas in the area can be measured.*

Radon home test kit

118 Og Oganesson

⊖ 118   ⊕ 118   ○ 177

State: **Solid**
Discovery: **2006**

Yuri Oganessian

The heaviest element yet made is oganesson. Scientists think it would be solid at room temperature, but it may really be an unreactive, noble gas. However, only a few atoms have been created so far, so its properties are not well understood. Oganesson was first produced by a team of Russian and American scientists who smashed californium and calcium atoms together at the **Joint Institute for Nuclear Research** in Dubna, Russia. The element was named after **Yuri Oganessian**, the leader of the team.

Joint Institute For Nuclear Research, Russia

Glossary

Acid
A compound that contains hydrogen, and releases ions of hydrogen when it is dissolved in water. These ions make acids very reactive.

Actinide
A member of a group of radioactive metals with relatively large atoms.

Alchemist
Person who experimented with chemicals before the science of chemistry began. Alchemists thought they could turn ordinary metals into gold.

Alkali
A compound that takes hydrogen ions from water molecules when it is dissolved in water. Alkalis react with acids.

Alkali metal
A group of metals that make alkalis when they react with water.

Alkaline earth metal
A group of metals that are found in nature, mainly in alkaline minerals.

Alloy
A material made by mixing a metal with tiny amounts of other metals or nonmetals. Steel is a common iron alloy used in buildings and railroads.

Artificial
Something that does not exist in nature. Several elements, including all that are heavier than uranium, are artificially produced by scientists in laboratories.

Atmosphere
The mixture of gases that surrounds a planet or moon. Earth's atmosphere is a mixture of nitrogen, oxygen, and argon, with tiny amounts of several other gases.

Atom
The smallest unit of an element. Atoms are composed of protons, neutrons, and electrons. The atoms of a particular element all have the same number of protons.

Atomic number
The number of protons in an atom of an element. Every element has a unique, unchanging atomic number.

Battery
A device containing chemicals that react to produce an electric current. There are two main kinds of battery: rechargeable and nonrechargeable.

Boiling point
The temperature at which a liquid gets hot enough to change into a gas.

Bond
The attraction between atoms that holds them together in an element or a compound.

Brittle
A way of describing a hard solid that shatters easily.

Carbonate
A compound that contains carbon and oxygen atoms, as well as atoms of other elements. Many minerals are carbonates.

Catalyst
A substance that speeds up a chemical reaction.

Chemist
A scientist who studies the elements, their compounds, and chemical reactions.

These vanadinite **crystals** contain the element vanadium.

Chemistry
The scientific study of the properties and reactions of the elements.

Chemical
Another word for a substance, generally meaning a compound made from several elements.

Combustion
A chemical reaction, involving oxygen, in which a fuel burns to produce heat and light in the form of flames.

Flames are the result of **combustion**.

Compound
A substance made of the atoms of one or more elements that are bonded together in a particular combination.

Conductor
A substance that lets heat or electricity flow easily through it.

Contract
To make or become smaller. Solids, liquids, and gases usually contract when the temperature goes down.

Corrosion
A chemical reaction that attacks a metal, or other solid object, usually due to the presence of oxygen and water.

Crystal

A naturally occurring solid substance whose atoms are arranged in a regular three dimensions pattern.

Decay

A process in which unstable atoms of radioactive elements break apart. The atoms of one element are transformed into those of another element during decay.

Density

The amount of matter held within a known volume of a material.

Dissolve

To become completely mixed into another substance. In most cases, a solid, such as salt, dissolves in a liquid, such as water.

Earthenware

A basic form of pottery, in which clay is heated to make it form hard structures.

Electrolysis

A process in which a compound is split into simpler substances using an electric current. Many elements, such as aluminum, are purified from their compounds in ores in this way.

Electrode

An electrical contact in an electric circuit. Electrodes can have a positive or negative charge.

Electron

A negatively charged particle inside an atom. Electrons orbit the atom's nucleus (or core) in layers called shells. They are also exchanged or shared by atoms to make bonds that hold molecules together.

Element

A pure substance that cannot be broken down into any simpler substances. Elements are the building blocks of matter. There are 118 known elements on Earth.

Expand

To make or become bigger. Solids, liquids, and gases usually expand when the temperature rises.

Fission

A process in which the nucleus of an unstable atom splits in two when it collides with a neutron. It releases more neutrons that start the cycle again, and this continues as a chain reaction. Many unstable nuclei undergo fission spontaneously, without being hit by a neutron. Fission releases a lot of energy. The process is used to generate electricity in nuclear power plants, and it can trigger atom bomb explosions.

Flammable

A way of describing anything that can catch fire easily.

Fusion

A process in which small atoms, such as those of hydrogen, are fused together with such force that they merge to form larger atoms, while releasing a lot of energy. The Sun is powered by the fusion of hydrogen atoms into helium in its central core.

Gas

A state in which the particles of matter (atoms or molecules) are not attached to each other, and move freely. A gas can flow, take any shape, and fill any container.

Group

A set of elements in a column in the periodic table. Elements in a group have similar properties because each atom has the same number of electrons in its outer shell.

Halogen

A member of a group near the far right of the periodic table. Halogens form salts with metals. They are reactive, nonmetallic elements.

Hardness

A measure of how easy it is to scratch or cut a substance with another substance.

Hydroxide

A type of compound containing hydrogen and oxygen, and normally a metallic element.

This is a chunk of ytterbium, a **lanthanide**.

Ion

An atom or a group of atoms that have an electric charge. While atoms have no overall charge, they become positive ions if they lose electrons or negative ions if they gain electrons.

Insulator

A substance that does not let heat or electricity flow easily through it.

Isotope

A form of an element with atoms that have the same number of protons but a different number of neutrons.

Lanthanide

A member of a set of metals with relatively large atoms. The elements in this series sit with the actinides, below the main part of the periodic table.

This **element** calcium is in crystal form.

Laser
A beam of light with a single wavelength, in which the waves are all perfectly lined up. Lasers are used in electronics and surgery.

Milk is a type of **mixture**.

LED
Short for light-emitting diode. An LED is a device that produces light when an electric current passes through it. The color of its light depends on the compounds used in it.

Liquid
A state in which the particles of matter (atoms or molecules) are only loosely attached to each other, and move freely. A liquid can flow and take any shape, but has a fixed volume.

Mass
The amount of matter in a substance.

Matter
The material that makes up everything around us.

Maglev
Short for magnetic levitation. This refers to some kinds of high-speed trains that use magnets to propel themselves while hovering over a track.

Magnet
A solid object that produces a magnetic field, which attracts certain materials to it and can attract or repel other magnets.

Magnetic
Relating to a magnet.

Magnetic field
The force field around a magnet.

Melting point
The temperature at which a solid gets hot enough to turn into a liquid.

Metal
A type of element that is likely to react by giving away the outermost electrons in its atoms. Most elements are metals, and they tend to be hard, shiny solids. Mercury is the only metal that is liquid at room temperature.

Mineral
A naturally occurring solid compound—or mixture of compounds—made up of different elements. Every mineral has particular characteristics, such as crystal shape and hardness. Minerals are mixed together to make the rocks in Earth's crust.

Mixture
A collection of substances that fill the same space but are not connected by chemical bonds. Examples of mixtures are seawater, milk, and mud. The contents of a mixture can be separated by a physical process, such as filtration.

Molecule
A single particle of a compound. Its two or more atoms are bonded together.

Neutron
A neutral particle in the nucleus of an atom. A neutron is about the same size as a proton but it does not have an electric charge.

Noble gases
A group of elements that are unreactive and generally form no compounds with the other elements. This is because the outermost shells in their atoms are filled with electrons. This group sits on the extreme right of the periodic table.

Nonmetal
A type of element that is likely to react by acquiring electrons in the outermost shell of its atoms. Nonmetals are usually crystalline solids, such as sulfur, or gases, such as oxygen. Bromine is the only nonmetal that is liquid at room temperature.

Nucleus
An atom's core, which contains its protons and neutrons. Nearly all the mass of an atom is packed into its nucleus.

Ore
A rock or mineral from which a useful element such as a metal can be purified and isolated.

Oxide
A compound in which oxygen is bound to one or more other elements.

Particle
A basic unit of which substances are made. Subatomic particles are units of which atoms are made including protons, neutrons, electrons, and many other smaller ones.

Particle accelerator
A machine in which atoms or subatomic particles are made to collide at high speeds. These collisions are then studied by scientists. Particle accelerators are used to produce artificial elements as well as study particles smaller than atoms. A cyclotron is a type of particle accelerator.

These petallike shapes may form when desert sand mixes with barite, an **ore** of barium.

Period
A set of elements in a row in the periodic table. Each atom of the elements in the first period have one electron shell. Atoms in the second period have two electron shells.

Periodic table
A table that identifies and classifies all known elements.

Photograph negative
A film or plate that has been exposed to light to show an image with reversed colors.

Photosynthesis
A complicated set of chemical reactions by which plants make their food. They use the energy of sunlight to convert water and carbon dioxide into sugar and oxygen.

Pollution
Harmful substances that are released into the environment. Pollution can be chemical—a gas, liquid, or solid added to the air, water, or soil.

Pressure
A measure of how hard a force pushes on a surface. Pressure depends upon the strength of the force and the area of the surface.

Proton
A positively charged particle in the nucleus of an atom. Protons attract electrons, and they circle the nucleus.

Radar
A system that detects the positions and speed of distant objects, such as aircraft.

Radiation
Energy released by atoms as light, infrared, ultraviolet (UV), and X-rays. The term "radiation" is also used to describe the rays given out by radioactive substances.

Radioactive
Describes a substance that contains unstable atoms, in which the nucleus breaks apart, or decays. When a nucleus decays, it releases at least one particle and its atomic number changes, so that the atom becomes a different element.

Reaction
A chemical process in which atoms or molecules form bonds with each other to form a new compound— or rearrange, to produce different compounds.

Renewable energy
A source of energy that will not run out, for example, wind.

Rust
The common name for the compounds that form when iron reacts with oxygen and water.

Salt
A compound that forms when an acid reacts with an alkali. Sodium chloride is the most familiar example of a salt.

Semimetal
An element that has properties of both metals and nonmetals.

Smelting
A chemical process that involves great heat in which a metal is extracted from its ore.

Solid
A state in which the particles of matter (atoms or molecules) are bound to each other, so they remain in fixed positions. A solid has a fixed shape and volume.

Stainless steel
An alloy of iron and carbon that also contains other metals, such as chromium, which stop the iron from rusting and increase its toughness.

Superconductor
A substance through which an electric current flows with no resistance; most substances resist the flow of electricity, and produce heat when current flows.

Synthetic
Another word for artificial. Out of the 118 known elements on Earth, more than 25 are synthetically made.

Toughness
A quality of a solid that shows how difficult it is to break. Steel is very tough— it may bend or twist, but is much harder to break.

Transition metal
A member of the set of metals that sit in the middle of the periodic table. Most metals belong to this set.

Toxic
Another word for poisonous or harmful.

Transparent
Another word for see-through. Glass, water, and air are transparent to light. Many materials are transparent to other forms of radiation.

Vacuum
An empty space that does not contain air or any other substance.

Vapor
A gas that can easily be changed back to a liquid by cooling it or putting it under pressure.

Verdigris
The green-gray layer that forms on copper when it comes in contact with air.

The Statue of Liberty is covered with a layer of **verdigris**.

Index

Laboratory sample of pure chromium

Diamond

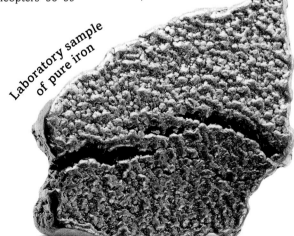
Laboratory sample of pure iron

Nickel balls

Laboratory sample of pure zinc

ACKNOWLEDGMENTS

The publisher would like to thank the following people for their help with making the book: Agnibesh Das, John Gillespie, Anita Kakkar, Sophie Parkes, Antara Raghavan, and Rupa Rao for editorial assistance; Revati Anand and Priyanka Bansal for design assistance; Vishal Bhatia for CTS assistance; Jeffrey E. Post, Ph.D. Chairman, Department of Mineral Sciences Curator, National Gem and Mineral Collection, National Museum of Natural History, Smithsonian; Kealy Gordon and Ellen Nanney from the Smithsonian Institution; Ruth O'Rourke for proofreading; Elizabeth Wise for indexing; and RGB Research Ltd (periodictable.co.uk), especially Dr. Max Whitby (Project Director), Dr Fiona Barclay (Business Development), Dr Ivan Timokhin (Senior Chemist), and Michal Miškolci (Production Chemist).

The publisher would like to thank the following for their kind permission to reproduce their photographs:

(Key: a-above; b-below/bottom; c-center; f-far; l-left; r-right; t-top)

9 Bridgeman Images: Golestan Palace Library, Tehran, Iran (cra). **Fotolia:** Malbert (ca). **Getty Images:** Gallo Images Roots Rf Collection / Clinton Friedman (fcla). **Wellcome Images http://creativecommons.org/licenses/by/4.0/:** (crb). **13 Getty Images:** Stockbyte (cra). **Science Photo Library:** Mcgill University, Rutherford Museum / Emilio Segre Visual Archives / American Institute Of Physics (crb). **15 Science Photo Library:** Sputnik (crb). **17 Alamy Stock Photo:** Dennis H. Dame (cr). **20 Dreamstime.com:** Alekc79 (cb). **NASA:** X-ray: NASA / CXC / Univ.Potsdam / L.Oskinova et al; Optical: NASA / STScI; Infrared: NASA / JPL-Caltech (cra). **21 Alamy Stock Photo:** Phil Degginger (cb); ULA (fcr). **NASA:** Bill Rodman (cla). **Science Photo Library:** U.S. Navy (crb). **24 Alamy Stock Photo:** PjrStudio (crb). **Dreamstime.com:** Titovstudio (ca). **naturepl.com:** Christophe Courteau (cr). **25 123RF.com:** Federico Cimino (cr). **Dreamstime.com:** Aleksey Boldin (cla); Bolygomaki (ca). **Getty Images:** Corbis (cla/mirror); Driendl Group (cb). **NASA:** (crb). **Science Photo Library. 26 123RF.com:** Stellargems (cra); Sara Winter (crb). **Dorling Kindersley:** Tim Parmenter / Natural History Museum, London (crb). **27 123RF.com:** Todsaporn Bunmuen (cl); Francis Dean (crb). **Alamy Stock Photo:** Artspace (cr); Hemis (c). **Dreamstime.com:** Abel Tumik (clb). **28-29 Alamy Stock Photo:** Hemis. **30 Alamy Stock Photo:** Siim Sepp (c). **31 123RF.com:** Petkov (ca). **Alamy Stock Photo:** Doug Steley B (cb). **Dorling Kindersley:** Dave King / The Science Museum, London (clb). **Dreamstime.com:** Mohammed Anwarul Kabir Choudhury (cr); Jarp3 (crb). **Getty Images:** John B. Carnett (c). **Science Photo Library:** CLAIRE PAXTON & JACQUI FARROW (cl). **32 123RF.com:** Dario Lo Presti (cra). **Getty Images:** De Agostini Picture Library (cr). **33 123RF.com:** Lenise Calleja (c/cracker); Chaiyaphong Kitphaephaisan (cr). **Alamy Stock Photo:** David J. Green (c). **Dreamstime.com:** Robert Semnic (cl). **Getty Images:** Stocktrek Images (cla). **Natural Resources Canada, Geological Survey of Canada:** (cb). **34 Dorling Kindersley:** Oxford University Museum of Natural History (cla). **Getty Images:** Ullstein Bild (clb); Universal Images Group (crb). **35 Alamy Stock Photo:** Universal Images Group North America LLC / DeAgostini (cla). **Getty Images:** Keystone-France (ca). **39 123RF.com:** Vladimir Kramin (crb). **Alamy Stock Photo:** Craig Wise (cla). **Dreamstime.com:** Studio306 (cla/sprinkler). **Getty Images:** fStop Images - Caspar Benson (cb). **NASA:** NASA / MSFC / David Higginbotham (c). **Science Photo Library:** David Parker (cr). **Wellcome Images http://creativecommons.org/licenses/by/4.0/:** Wellcome Library (cra). **40 Dorling Kindersley:** Colin Keates / Natural History Museum, London (cla). **41 123RF.com:** Thodonal (cb). **Alamy Stock Photo:** Mohammed Anwarul Kabir Choudhury (clb/cement); Dominic Harrison (cla); Phil Degginger (clb). **Dreamstime.com:** Nu1983 (cr); Marek Uliasz (cra). **Getty Images:** Yoshikazu Tsuno (crb). **Rex by Shutterstock:** Neil Godwin / Future Publishing (cl). **42 Alamy Stock Photo:** Phil Degginger (cl). **Dorling Kindersley:** Natural History Museum, London (clb); Holts Gems (cla). **43 123RF.com:** Oksana Tkachuk (c). **Alamy Stock Photo:** Ekasit Wangprasert (cb). **Dreamstime.com:** Waxart (cr). **44-45 Alamy Stock Photo:** Inge Johnsson. **47 123RF.com:** Anatol Adutskevich (cra); Paweł Szczepa⊠ski (ca); Ronstik (crb). **Dorling Kindersley:** Durham University Oriental Museum (cla). **Dreamstime.com:** Showface (cr). **iStockphoto.com:** Lamiel (cl). **48-49 Alamy Stock Photo:** The Natural History Museum (cb). **49 123RF.com:** Roman Ivaschenko (cr); Wiesław Jarek (ca). **Getty Images:** DEA / S. VANNINI (c). **Science Photo Library:** ALAIN POL, ISM (crb). **51 Getty Images:** Heritage Images (cra). **Science Photo Library:** Public Health England (ca, crb); Public Health England (cb). **54 123RF.com:** Stocksnapper (cb). **Alamy Stock Photo:** Universal Images Group North America LLC / DeAgostini (cra). **Dreamstime.com:** Dimitar Marinov (crb). **55 123RF.com:** Leonid Pilnik (fcra); Sergei Zhukov (cr). **Alamy Stock Photo:** Military Images (cra); Hugh Threlfall (fcrb). **Dreamstime.com:** Flynt (crb). **56 123RF.com:** Mykola Davydenko (clb); Kaetana (crb). **Alamy Stock Photo:** Shawn Hempel (cl). **57 Alamy Stock Photo:** imageBROKER (crb). **Dorling Kindersley:** Natural History Museum, London (cr). **58 Alamy Stock Photo:** Vincent Ledvina (clb). **59 123RF.com:** Chaiyaphong Kitphaephaisan (c/rail); lightboxx (c); Tawat Langnamthip (crb). **Alamy Stock Photo:** Hemis (cb); B.A.E. Inc. (ca). **Dreamstime.com:** Nexus7 (cr). **Getty Images:** Michael Nicholson (cra). **60 123RF.com:** Serezniy (clb). **Getty Images:** Detlev van Ravenswaay (cl). **61 Alamy Stock Photo:** PhotoCuisine RF (c); SERDAR (l). **Dorling Kindersley:** Doubleday Holbeach Depot (cra). **Dreamstime.com:** Igor Sokolov (clb). **Science Photo Library:** Jim West (cr). **62-63 123RF.com:** Wang Aizhong. **64 Alamy Stock Photo:** Susan E. Degginger (crb); The Natural History Museum (cr). **65 Dorling Kindersley:** Rolls Royce Heritage Trust (cl). **Dreamstime.com:** Margojh (c). **Getty Images:** Pascal Preti (cb); Science & Society Picture Library (cla). **66 Alamy Stock Photo:** Alan Curtis / LGPL (ca). **67 123RF.com:** Psvrusso (ca); Евгений Косцов (crb). **Alamy Stock Photo:** INTERFOTO (fcla). **Dorling Kindersley:** National Music Museum (cla). **Getty Images:** Fanthomme Hubert (cra). **68 Alamy Stock Photo:** Jeff Rotman (crb). **Dorling Kindersley:** Natural History Museum, London (ca); Oxford University Museum of Natural History (clb). **69 123RF.com:** Dilyana Kruseva (cr); Vitaliy Kytayko (cla); Photopips (crb). **Alamy Stock Photo:** Paul Ridsdale Pictures (tc). **Dorling Kindersley:** University of Pennsylvania Museum of Archaeology and Anthropology (cb). **70-71 Alamy Stock Photo:** Novarc Images. **72 Alamy Stock Photo:** Phil Degginger (cla). **73 Alamy Stock Photo:** PjrStudio (clb). **Dreamstime.com:** Sean Pavone (cra). **NASA. 74 Dorling Kindersley:** Oxford University Museum of Natural History (cla). **75 123RF.com:** Belchonock (cr); Weerayos Surareangchai (cla). **Alamy Stock Photo:** dpa picture alliance (ca); Georgios Kollidas (cra); PNWL (cl). **Getty Images:** SSPL (cb). **Science Photo Library:** David Parker (crb). **76 123RF.com:** Okan Akdeniz (clb); Nevarpp (fclb); Andriy Popov (crb). **Dreamstime.com:** Ryan Stevenson (cb). **77 123RF.com:** Mohammed Anwarul Kabir Choudhury (cra); Vladimir Nenov (crb). **Alamy Stock Photo:** The Natural History Museum (cl). **NASA. 78 Alamy Stock Photo:** Oleksandr Chub (crb); The Natural History Museum (ca). **Science Photo Library. 78-79 Alamy Stock Photo:** Susan E. Degginger (c); epa european pressphoto agency b.v. (cb). **79 Science Photo Library:** David Parker (crb); Rvi Medical Physics, Newcastle / Simon Fraser (cr). **80 123RF.com:** Missisya (cb); Darren Pullman (clb). **Alamy Stock Photo:** GFC Collection (crb). **81 123RF.com:** Hywit Dimyadi (cra). **Dreamstime.com:** Shutterman99 (ca). **Getty Images:** Alain Nogues (crb). **82 Alamy Stock Photo:** Greenshoots Communications (ca); PjrStudio (crb). **Dreamstime.com:** Robert Chlopas (cr). **Science Photo Library. 83 123RF.com:** Dmitry Lobanov (crb); Jose Ignacio Soto (tr); Valerii Zan (cr). **Dreamstime.com:** Maloy40 (ca). **Getty Images:** Paul Taylor (cl). **84 Getty Images:** DEA / PHOTO 1 (clb); DEA / G.CIGOLINI (cl). **85 Alamy Stock Photo:** David J. Green (cra); Chromorange / Juergen Wiesler (crb). **Dorling Kindersley:** The University of Aberdeen (ca). **Dreamstime.com:** Stephanie Frey (cla); Gaurav Masand (cl). **Getty Images:** Science & Society Picture Library (clb). **Science Photo Library. 86 123RF.com:** Serhii Kucher (crb). **Alamy Stock Photo:** Ableimages (crb/micro). **Dreamstime.com:** Michal Baranski (cra). **Getty Images:** Lester V. Bergman (cra). **Science Photo Library. 87 Dreamstime.com:** Andrey Eremin (clb). **Science Photo Library. 88 123RF.com:** Ludinko (cra). **Getty Images:** Trisha Leeper (crb). **89 123RF.com:** Akulamatiau (crb); Anton Starikov (clb). **Dreamstime.com:** Homydesign (cb). **90 Alamy Stock Photo:** Antony Nettle (crb). **Dreamstime.com:** Farbled (c); Vesna Njagulj (clb). **91 Alamy Stock Photo:** Science (cra). **Dreamstime.com:** Reddogs (crb). **Science Photo Library:** Dr Gopal Murti (ca); Dirk Wiersma (cla). **92 Alamy Stock Photo:** Citizen of the Planet (crb). **Getty Images:** Yva Momatiuk and John Eastcott (cra). **Science Photo Library. 93 123RF.com:** Sergey Jarochkin (crb); mg154 (cl). **Alamy Stock Photo:** Pictorial Press Ltd (clb). **NASA:** CXC / NGST (ca). **94 Dorling Kindersley:** Natural History Museum, London (r). **Science Photo Library:** Natural History Museum, London (l). **95 Alamy Stock Photo:** Four sided triangle (c); I studio (ca); Friedrich Saurer (cb). **Dreamstime.com:** Adamanto (cr). **Getty Images:** PHAS (cra); Royal Photographic Society (cl). **Science Photo Library:** Dr P. Marazzi (fcr); National Physical Laboratory (C) Crown Copyright (cla); Sovereign / Ism (crb). **96 Science Photo Library:** Science Stock Photography (cra). **97 123RF.com:** Ratchaphon Chaihuai (clb). **Dorling Kindersley:** Alistair Duncan / Cairo Museum (ca); Barnabas Kindersley (cl). **Dreamstime.com:** Nastya81 (crb); Scanrail (c). **Getty Images:** Charles O'Rear (fcrb); John Phillips (cr). **magiccarpics.co.uk:** Robert George (cb). **NASA. 98-99 Alamy Stock Photo:** imageBROKER. **101 123RF.com:** Teerawut Masawat (cla). **Getty Images:** Science & Society Picture Library (ca); Science & Society Picture Library (cr). **Paul Hickson, The University of British Columbia:** (clb). **102 Getty Images:** Bettmann (cla). **Science Photo Library:** Ernest Orlando Lawrence Berkeley National Laboratory / Emilio Segre Visual Archives / American Institute Of Physics (clb). **103 Alamy Stock Photo:** Peter van Evert (crb); Randsc (clb). **Science Photo Library:** Lawrence Berkeley National Laboratory (cr). **104 Science Photo Library:** David Parker (clb); Wheeler Collection / American Institute Of Physics (cla); David Parker (cb). **105 Alamy Stock Photo:** imageBROKER (cla). **Science Photo Library:** Emilio Segre Visual Archives / American Institute Of Physics (cb). **106 Alamy Stock Photo:** Granger Historical Picture Archive (cb). **Science Photo Library:** David Parker (cla). **107 Alamy Stock Photo:** Sherab (cl). **Science Photo Library:** Dung Vo Trung / Look At Sciences (cr). **110 123RF.com:** Oleksandr Marynchenko (clb); Naruedom Yaempongsa (crb). **Alamy Stock Photo:** John Cancalosi (cla); Reuters (cb). **111 123RF.com:** Cobalt (cra); Veniamin Kraskov (cra/red). **Dreamstime.com:** Akulamatiau (cb). **Science Photo Library. 112 Alamy Stock Photo:** Everett Collection Historical (crb). **113 Alamy Stock Photo:** Ivan Vdovin (crb). **Fotolia:** Efired (cra). **114 Rex by Shutterstock:** (crb). **Science Photo Library:** Pr Michel Brauner, ISM (cra). **115 Alamy Stock Photo:** G M Thomas (cr). **Science Photo Library:** Patrick Llewelyn-Davies (crb). **116 123RF.com:** Vereshchagin Dmitry (br); Vitalii Tiahunov (cra); Vitalii Tiahunov (fcra). **117 123RF.com:** Preecha Bamrungrai (crb). **Dreamstime.com:** Hxdbzxy (cra). **120 Alamy Stock Photo:** Yon Marsh (br). **ESA:** (cra). **Science Photo Library:** Dirk Wiersma (clb). **121 Alamy Stock Photo:** Mike Greenslade (l). **Science Photo Library:** Trevor Clifford Photography (cra); Sputnik (crb). **122 Alamy Stock Photo:** Derrick Alderman (cr). **Science Photo Library:** J.C. REVY, ISM (cra); Lawrence Berkeley Laboratory (crb). **123 NASA:** NASA / JPL-Caltech / Malin Space Science Systems (cra). **Science Photo Library:** Thedore Gray, Visuals Unlimited (ca). **124 Alamy Stock Photo:** Randsc (crb). **Dreamstime.com:** Marcorubino (clb). **NASA. Science Photo Library:** Science Source (cla). **125 Alamy Stock Photo:** 501 collection (cla). **Getty Images:** George Rinhart (clb). **Science Photo Library:** US Department Of Energy (ca). **126 Science Photo Library:** American Institute Of Physics (cra); Sputnik (cb); Sputnik (clb). **127 Alamy Stock Photo:** Granger Historical Picture Archive (clb). **Science Photo Library:** Ernest Orlando Lawrence Berkeley National Laboratory / Emilio Segre Visual Archives / American Institute Of Physi (ca). **130 123RF.com:** Terry Davis (cla). **Alamy Stock Photo:** Chris stock photography (fcra). **130-131 Alamy Stock Photo:** Universal Images Group North America LLC / DeAgostini (cb). **131 123RF.com:** Sirichai Asawalapsakul (ca); Joerg Hackemann (cla); Wilawan Khasawong (ca/boric); Michał Giel (c/TV). **Alamy Stock Photo:** Chronicle (fcra). **Dorling Kindersley:** Tank Museum (crb). **Fotolia:** L_amica (c); Alex Staroseltsev (cr). **Getty Images:** Heritage Images (cra). **132 Science Photo Library:** Dirk Wiersma (ca). **133 123RF.com:** Destinacigdem (cla); Olaf Schulz (cb). **Dreamstime.com:** Apple Watch Edition™ is a trademark of Apple Inc., registered in the U.S. and other countries. (cr); Stepan Popov (cl); Simon Gurney (fcr); Zalakdagli (clb). **134-135 Getty Images:** Brasil2. **136 123RF.com:** Martin Lehmann (c). **Alamy Stock Photo:** BSIP SA (cra). **Getty Images:** Visuals Unlimited, Inc. / GIPhotoStock (cra/disc). **NASA. 137 123RF.com:** Norasit Kaewsai (cb/trans); Ouhdesire (clb); Dmytro Sukharevskyy (cb). **Dreamstime.com:** Christian Delbert (crb). **138 Dreamstime.com:** Monika Wisniewska (cl). **Getty Images:** Science & Society Picture Library (cr). **139 123RF.com:** Fotana (clb). **Alamy Stock Photo:** Stock Connection Blue (cla). **Getty Images:** The Asahi Shimbun (cr). **142 Alamy Stock Photo:** Pablo Paul (cra); WidStock (cla). **Dorling Kindersley:** Natural History Museum (crb); Natural History Museum (fcra). **143 123RF.com:** Oleksii Sergieiev (crb). **Alamy Stock Photo:** David J. Green (cla); Image.com (ca). **Dorling Kindersley:** National Cycle Collection (ca/cycle); The Science Museum, London (fcrb). **144-145 Bridgeman Images:** Christie's Images. **146 123RF.com:** Danilo Forcellini (fcrb). **Alamy Stock Photo:** Phil Degginger (cra); Perry van Munster (crb). **147 123RF.com:** Scanrail (ca). **Alamy Stock Photo:** MixPix (cla); Haiyin Wang (crb). **Dreamstime.com:** Halil I. Inci (fcrb). **Getty Images:** Handout (cr). **Science Photo Library:** Lawrence Berkeley National Laboratory (cb). **148 123RF.com:** Viktoriya Chursina (cra). **Dreamstime.com:** Bright (crb); Oleksandr Lysenko (cr). **Getty Images:** DEA / G. CIGOLINI (cla). **149 123RF.com:** Lapis2380 (cb). **150 Alamy Stock Photo:** Sarah Brooksby (cb). **Dorling Kindersley:** Natural History Museum, London (cla). **151 123RF.com:** Vira Dobosh (clb). **Science Photo Library:** Sputnik (cr); Sputnik (cl). **154 Science Photo Library:** Dr.Jeremy Burgess (clb). **155 123RF.com:** Mohammed Anwarul Kabir Choudhury (cra/color); Teerawut Masawat (cla); David Gilbert (ca). **Alamy Stock Photo:** Lyroky (cr); Tim Scrivener (crb). **NASA:** JPL (cra). **156-157 Getty Images:** Icon Sports Wire. **158 Dorling Kindersley:** Natural History Museum, London (cr/beaker). **Dreamstime.com:** Tomas Pavelka (c). **Getty Images:** Auscape (ca). **158-159 Science Photo Library. 159 123RF.com:** Action sports (cb); De2marco (c); Arina Zaiachin (clb); Mohammed Anwarul Kabir Choudhury (crb). **Getty Images:** Simone Brandt (cr). **160 123RF.com:** Maksym Yemelyanov (crb). **Alamy Stock Photo:** Andrew Ammendolia (fclb). **Dreamstime.com:** Jaggat (clb); Science Pics (ca). **161 Dreamstime.com:** Chris Boswell (cra). **Getty Images:** SuperStock (cb). **Science Photo Library:** Phil Degginger (cla); Phil Degginger (fcla). **162 Dorling Kindersley:** Harry Taylor (cla). **163 123RF.com:** Serezniy (c). **Dreamstime.com:** Ericlefrancais (cla); Bert Folsom (clb). **Science Photo Library:** Sputnik (cr). **166 123RF.com:** Kameel (clb); Russ McElroy (cra). **167 123RF.com:** Rostislav Ageev (cra/diver). **Alamy Stock Photo:** PhotoAlto (crb); RGB Ventures / SuperStock (fcr). **Dreamstime.com:** Narin Phapnam (cb); Uatp1 (cl). **Getty Images:** STR (clb). **SuperStock:** Cultura Limited / Cultura Limited (cra). **168 123RF.com:** Cseh Ioan (clb). **Alamy Stock Photo:** Big Pants Productions (cb). **Science Photo Library:** Farrell Grehan (cra). **168-169 Alamy Stock Photo:** The Natural History Museum (ca). **169 123RF.com:** Lucian Milasan (crb); Nikkytok (c). **Alamy Stock Photo:** Krys Bailey (clb); Paul Felix Photography (cra). **Dreamstime.com:** Nfransua (ca); Kirsty Pargeter (cla); Olha Rohulya (cb). **170-171 Getty Images:** Kazuyoshi Nomachi. **172 123RF.com:** Maksym Bondarchuk (crb); Sauletas (cb). **Dreamstime.com:** Orijinal (clb). **Science Photo Library:** Dirk Wiersma (cra). **173 123RF.com:** Jiri Vaclavek (ca). **Alamy Stock Photo:** Hugh Threlfall (fcra); Universal Images Group North America LLC / DeAgostini (cla). **Getty Images:** Steve Proehl (crb). **174 Alamy Stock Photo:** Dan Leeth (clb). **175 Alamy Stock Photo:** CPC Collection (cb); Sputnik (cla). **178 Dorling Kindersley:** Natural History Museum, London (crb); Oxford University Museum of Natural History (cla). **179 123RF.com:** Kirill Krasnov (c); Chaovarut Sthoop (clb). **Alamy Stock Photo:** The Print Collector (cra); World History Archive (cl); World foto (cr). **Dreamstime.com:** Bogdan Dumitru (fcrb); Stephan Pietzko (cla). **Getty Images:** John B. Carnett (crb). **181 123RF.com:** Sergey Jarochkin (c); Dmitry Naumov (cr); Hxdbzxy (cb, cb/bleach). **Alamy Stock Photo:** Maksym Yemelyanov (crb). **Dorling Kindersley:** Thackeray Medical Museum (cl). **182-183 Science Photo Library:** Alexis Rosenfeld. **184-185 Getty Images:** George Steinmetz (cb). **Science Photo Library:** Charles D. Winters (c). **185 Dreamstime.com:** Jose Manuel Gelpi Diaz (crb); Larry Finn (ca). **Science Photo Library. 186 123RF.com:** Alexandr Malyshev (fcra); ⊠ ⊠⊠ (cra). **Alamy Stock Photo:** BSIP SA (crb). **187 Science Photo Library:** Union Carbide Corporation's Nuclear Division, courtesy EMILIO SEGRE VISUAL ARCHIVES, Physics Today Collection / AMERICAN INSTITUTE OF PHYSICS (crb). **190-191 Dreamstime.com:** Andrey Navrotskiy (b). **190 123RF.com:** Leonid Ikan (cb). **© CERN:** (cra). **191 Dreamstime.com:** Yinan Zhang (cb). **iStockphoto.com:** Gobigpicture (t). **Science Photo Library:** Brian Bell (ca); Patrick Landmann (crb). **192-193 Getty Images:** Rolf Geissinger / Stocktrek Images. **194 123RF.com:** Rainer Albiez (cra). **Alamy Stock Photo:** D. Hurst (crb). **Science Photo Library:** Andrew Lambert Photography (clb). **195 Dreamstime.com:** Stocksolutions (cr). **Getty Images:** Floris Leeuwenberg (cra); Mario Tama (clb). **Science Photo Library:** Crown Copyright / Health & Safety Laboratory (crb). **196 Dorling Kindersley:** Clive Streeter / The Science Museum, London (crb). **Dreamstime.com:** Liouthe (cra). **Getty Images:** Genya Savilov (fcra). **Science Photo Library:** (cb). **197 123RF.com:** Alexlmx (fcrb). **Alamy Stock Photo:** Alexandru Nika (crb). **Dreamstime.com:** Jultud (clb). **Getty Images:** Brand X Pictures (cra). **NASA:** JPL-Caltech (cb). **198 Science Photo Library:** Dirk Wiersma (ca). **199 123RF.com:** Nmint (cl). **Alamy Stock Photo:** ITAR-TASS Photo Agency (cra); Gordon Mills (cla); RGB Ventures / SuperStock (clb); ITAR-TASS Photo Agency (crb). **200 Alamy Stock Photo:** Shawn Hempel (bc). **205 Dorling Kindersley:** Natural History Museum (cla)

All other images © Dorling Kindersley
For further information see: **www.dkimages.com**